Paw Prints On Your Heart

Basic Obedience

For Your New Puppy Or Rescue

Or

How To Train Your New Companion

To Become The Dog You Want To Live With

Paw Prints On Your Heart

Basic Obedience

For Puppies And Rescues

Joyce Guthrie

Publisher

Paw Prints On Your Heart

ISBN 978-1-300-47758-7

Printed in the United States Of America

Front cover design by

Joyce Guthrie

Printed and bound by

http://www.Lulu.com

Dedication

For all their hard work and dedication to Great Dane Rescue, and for the suggestion that this book was necessary, this book is dedicated to Janet and Lourdes.

Because of Janet's suggestion to write this book, $1 of every sale will go to Great Dane rescue, unless another rescue organization is specified.

I would also like to dedicate this book to all those that have opened their hearts and homes to a rescue. It takes a little more intestinal fortitude-at times-to take on an older rescue, one with a few scars, or a few health issues, but one still with years to offer and a lot of love to give.

Contents:

Chapter 1

Picking Your Puppy Or Rescue

There are several common pitfalls when people go to pick the companion with which they plan to spend many joy filled years. The first is to allow the animal to "pick them." I cannot stress enough how many times this has become the puppy or rescue from hell. The outgoing individual is, many times, merely an out of control individual and as such requires a skilled trainer with patience, room for the individual to expend the excess energy, in other words; a job, energy to match that of the rescue and a facility in which to get all of this accomplished. The average person or family looking for a companion is not quite up to the task, nor are they interested in this much work. Once they get said rescue or puppy home and the issue rears its ugly head, they have fallen in love with the rescue/puppy, now have their hands full and will be spending many hours and dollars working to train/retrain the companion they had hoped to bring home and enjoy. There will be many tears cried in frustration, deliberations over whether they should keep the dear one or give it up, feeling like a failure(s), all of which is unnecessary if only they had not allowed the rescue/puppy to pick them.

Before going to visit rescues or puppies, people rarely ever stop to consider what their strengths and weaknesses are let alone write them down. People need to be aware of what their limitations are, as well as their strengths BEFORE they go to see the rescues. In this way they will not be tempted to take on more than they can handle or pass on an individual that might be their perfect match due to an issue that they truly might not be overwhelmed by.

I advocate sitting and making a list of issues that you find difficult to deal with and those that you would not struggle with. Split a page down the middle and one side write acceptable and on he other not acceptable. For example, if you have never felt it was difficult to house break a rescue or puppy, or that cleaning up after one that took longer than the average to house break was not a problem for you, put that on your list of acceptable issues. If leash training a rescue that was a bad puller was easy for you, put that one down on he list under acceptable issues. If you have always had trouble training leash pullers, put that one down under unacceptable issues instead. If your daily schedule is such that you can handle a rescue with separation anxiety issues, there is another one for the acceptable column, if your situation is not, list that as a problem under the unacceptable column. If you have a back issue, rescues needing physical assistance for some reason are not on your list of acceptable. If you live in a home with a couple of strapping young teenage kids, strong spouse and you are also in good shape, you may be more comfortable adding rescues with physical challenges to your list. If you live in an area that does not allow fenced yards, a deaf rescue should be excluded. Understand that a rescues' issues can be physical, emotional or behavioral. They can require a commitment from you that can mean your time, finances, and skills for either a short or long term

These are just a few examples, but this is what I am talking about. Look to find a rescue that matches your physical, financial and emotional abilities, your goals and your level of training abilities. Whether you are looking for a rescue or puppy one method that can be used to determine the particulars in the personality of your potential companion, to help take some of the guess work out of it for you, is to do what is called PAT testing, or Puppy Aptitude Testing. Although this is designed for puppies at 7 weeks of age, it can also easily be used for older puppies or rescues, I use it for testing potential service rescues and their ages range anywhere from 6 months to a year old. There are a few things that can be a little more difficult when testing older rescues, especially if you are testing a large breed, but those parts of the test can be modified. The point of the test is that it will give you a very comprehensive idea of the personality of the rescue/puppy. I would recommend my book PAT Testing To Pick The Perfect Puppy to gain a full understanding of how to perform the test as well as how to interpret the results. In short, PAT testing will let you know if the individual is physically tough or soft, emotionally tough or soft, socially dominant or submissive, whether or not they are sound sensitive, sensitive to sights, whether or not they have a strong prey drive and whether or not they have a natural retrieval skill. Although this final statement doesn't seem applicable when looking for a companion, the test for retrieval skills also reveals the willingness of the individual to work with humans. All of this information, each section of the test and how each relates to the other can give you a very comprehensive idea about the potential companion and allow you to make a more intelligent and less emotional choice. **There are no imperfect puppies or rescues, only imperfect matches**. If the match is right for both canine and human, both will be happy. You need to understand that if you are not happy ultimately with the match, neither is your canine companion. It is for this reason-not only for your happiness in finding the correct match, but for the rescue/puppy as well-that finding that just right match is so imperative.

Chapter Two

The First Two Weeks

The first two weeks that your new companion is in your home are critical for shaping future behavior. What you establish as "okay" in the first two weeks will be what will be the guidelines your new companion will look to continue to emulate for the following years the two of you spend together. There are a number of things that need to be established in these first two weeks and then adhered to from then on. These start with house training, progress to establishing a yard, deciding whether or not your companion will be allowed in bed, on furniture, where they will be fed and when, and the list goes on.

The first thing you need to do is fill your pocket with cookies. This can be anything from small pieces of kibble to strips of Pupperoni-the generic stuff works just fine, to the Bil-Jac treats or anything that will easily stay in your pocket and not get mushy.

You need to memorize the Four P's Of Positive Puppy Training:

Praise, Patience, Persistence, Practice

There is no place for Punishment in Training.

This is not to say that at some point corrections cannot be implemented as a part of the training regimen; there are many different methods of training. Some methods use only positive motivation, some use both positive and negative, methods, and some use mainly positive, but also mild corrections when necessary. I do not use any corrections when training puppies or new exercises to any rescue. I do not feel you can correct a rescue or puppy for making a mistake when they do not yet "know" the exercise. Later on in the training process, once the exercise is known and understood, there may be times when they do the exercise incorrectly or choose not to do it. It is at these times that corrections may be warranted. Each rescue/puppy is different, and as such there are those for which lack of praise is the harshest correction they will ever need. When I say correction I do not mean punishment, there is a big difference between the two. Just like a road has two shoulders, training should be a road that is just as clearly defined. It is for this reason that I do feel that corrections are acceptable. I think rescues, as well as puppies, feel comfortable knowing where "both shoulders" on the road are located. They tend not to like gray areas. Again, corrections have no place in initial training; you cannot correct a rescue or puppy for what they are learning, only after they know an exercise. The choice of severity of correction needs to be tempered by the temperament of the individual rescue/puppy. Keep in mind that lack of praise is a valid correction and serves the purpose when warranted. Other rescues may need a slight collar pop correction, or merely a verbal "angh, angh" will suffice. There are a few other specific corrections for more advanced training-retrieval work; the ear pinch, tapping under the chin, etc., (these are what I would term severe corrections and ones I would not use under normal circumstances with the majority of my Danes or service dogs I have in training), that may have a place and time; however, these have no place in puppy training. Training is about establishing a relationship with your rescue or puppy. You want this relationship to be based on positive experiences. There is also a school of thought that is positive, but not reward based, if you will. The thought process is simple, you are the alpha, the pack leader and the pack leader does not "give up the food". I do not train to establish dominance and I do not have to be dominant to "rule my pack" as it were. A true alpha rules with a velvet glove-or paw if you will and is more like royalty. There is no force and there is no sense of dominance that has to be established. If your dogs do not respect you, withholding treats in training is not going to make one bit of difference. If you think of it in terms of Queen Elizabeth walking into a room: She is given respect merely by her presence, she does not have to do anything to exert force, she just IS. Giving commands in a voice of authority, not as a question, not begging or whining will make a difference. Rewarding the correct response will encourage your companion to want to respond again-and more quickly. Rewarding with cookies is only part of the reward. The whole reward is also verbal and physical praise. What you need to remember is that you will not always have cookies on hand, but you will always have your voice and hands to praise and encourage your companion. As your training progresses, the food treats will become intermittent to the point that they are only occasional-you will be fading them out-but the verbal and physical praise will always be present. To that end, they are an aid in initial training, nothing more, nothing less. Food is not a symbol of your dominance; offering your companion treats as a reward does not lesson their respect for you, nor does is lesson your status in the "pack". It will, however, assist your companion in finding the correct positions without using force, encourage your companion to work for you and they will be eagerly looking forward to the next training session. Your verbal and physical praise should not be underestimated and should not be replaced with the food rewards. In the beginning all three are used together to achieve the desired result. As time goes on, and your companion begins to catch on, food rewards will be faded out as a lure and as a reward and your praise will be all that is necessary. Dominance will have never been lost or gained or ever even have come into question. Training will have been accomplished on a positive note. Your companion will have gained respect and admiration for you while the two of you were building the most wonderful relationship you can ever imagine.

CATCH THEM DOING SOMETHING RIGHT

With your pocket full of cookies, you have a puppy or rescue that is unsure of whether or not they live with you or if they are just a guest. It is up to you in these first few days/weeks to make them feel at home and loved. Food is generally the way to any 4-legggers' heart! You want them to feel at home, but at the same time you are establishing the house rules, so you must be firm in what you will allow for the rest of their life and what you will not allow. Everyone in the house needs to be on board and following the same set of rules. If the puppy/rescue is not going to be allowed on the furniture, everyone needs to be consistent in not allowing this to happen, if they are going to be allowed to sleep in bed with someone, then everyone needs to be in agreement on this as well. If they are not to be allowed in certain rooms, keep those doors closed, or baby gates in place. If you don't want them counter surfing, keep food and toys off of the counters, remember; you are the intelligent thinking one. Do not leave temptation out in plain sight or smell. Try to think of each situation in the same terms with which your new companion will be using. Here they are in a new environment. They have a very keen sense of smell. They are drawn to something on the counter. What they are thinking is simple. "How wonderful these humans have left me this special gift. How smart of me to have found it. I'll have to continue to check this location in the future for something tasty again." You have set the precedent for counter surfing.

Remember when telling your puppy they are not allowed to do something that the negative needs to be quickly followed by a positive. For example, if my puppy starts to try to climb on the couch because that is where I am, I will gently push them off, giving the command, "off", and then praising them, both physically and verbally and by giving them a food treat, when all 4 paws are back on the floor. THEN, and this is important, knowing that the reason they wanted to get up on the couch was to be with me, I will follow all of this with getting down on the floor with my puppy and giving them 15 minutes of play time. Depending on how long it has been since they were out to potty, I might also take them outside-just in case. What is important to note here, is that many people will discipline the puppy/rescue for attempting to get on the couch.

They do not follow it up with praise for getting off as requested, this is mistake number one. They then do not acknowledge the reason the puppy/rescue wanted to get up there to start with-to be with this person, this savior, the one that makes them feel safe and loved. They are then ignored. This generally leads to said puppy/rescue getting into something they are not supposed to, getting attention-negative though it might be, it is still attention and that is after all what they were after to start with-mission accomplished?

Taking 15 minutes to enjoy your newly acquired companion is well worth the effort. It will instill in them they are loved and this is their new home, they are not a guest and it will keep them out of trouble.

There are many ways to help your new puppy/rescue feel at home. Catching them doing something right is one of the best ways to help them in this manner. **You will become a cookie PEZ dispenser.** If you see your puppy/rescue sitting, run over to them and give them a cookie and say, "good sit". If you see them in a down, repeat the same process. If they are standing, again, repeat the same process. If they are coming toward you and you are sure they are committed, use their name and "come". When they get to you, give tons of praise and cookies and have a big party. Let your puppy/rescue know that they have done a super wonderful thing coming to you. This is an informal recall.

Coming to your home is a new, somewhat frightening, but at the same time intriguing experience. You want to do everything you can to make it a positive experience.

SCHEDULE

You want to establish a schedule as soon as you get your puppy/rescue home and settled in. If you know what time your puppy/rescue was used to getting up, being fed, etc., that information is helpful in that you can start with similar times and adjust them in 30 minute increments until you have them on your time schedule. If you do not have access to this information, start them on your schedule, but do not be alarmed if they have a little trouble adapting in the beginning. Meal times may be the hardest for them. They may not be hungry when you have time for them to eat, so they may not clean up their bowl and you may be tempted to leave it down for them. Just offer it to them again at the next feeding. They will adapt to the new schedule. The sooner you get the new schedule established the better off all of you will be.

You will want to keep a record of your puppy/rescues potty habits, sleep habits, play time habits, eating habits etc., in the beginning. This will help you establish where any problem areas may be. For example, you may have a problem getting them to eat in the morning and find that they are very active at night and prefer to eat later at night and sleep later in the morning. I had one Dane that was never keen on breakfast. I feed my Danes 3 times a day, but instead of breakfast, lunch and dinner, she had lunch, dinner and "forth meal". She was not a fat Dane, she was always lean, all muscle and bone, she was an athletic Dane, loved agility and tracking, so the lesser weight was suited to her sleeker body.

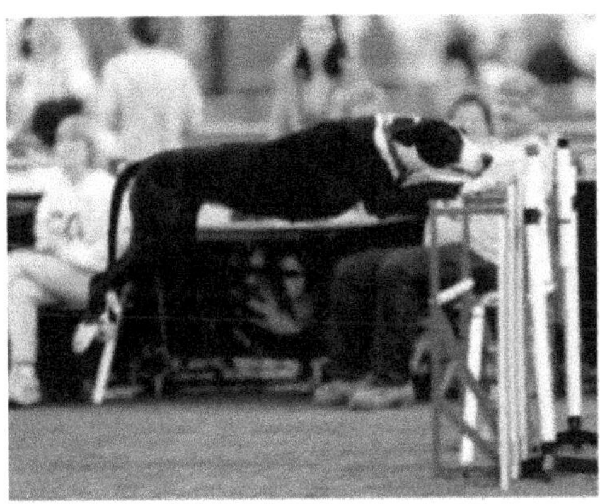

Jasmine in agility-and yes, she cleared this one easily!

If you find your puppy/rescue is going through a growth spurt and needs more than the average amount, you may need to split the feedings into 4 meals instead of 3. This may be especially true if your rescue comes to you slightly under weight or if they are a picky eater when they first arrive. Feeding smaller more frequent meals may be the key to getting their appetite stimulated as well as a slow and gradual weight gain. Hopefully being a picky eater will be only temporary. Depending on your breed(s) once they become an adult you can usually go to 2 feedings a day. With the large and giant breeds you may want to continue with 3 feeding for life, depending on the amount of food they need. I never like to feed more than 3 cups per feeding. If they need more than 6 cups per day, I will stay with 3 feedings per day. Many small toys, on the other hand can manage quite well with 1 feeding per day.

Keeping track of when your puppy/rescue is most active will let you know when you can catch your puppy/rescue at the most active/attentive and thus the best time for training. Keeping your training sessions short, 5-10 minutes in the beginning, will keep your puppy/rescue from getting bored. You can have several of these sessions per day.

The other thing that is going to weigh heavily into your schedule is the potty schedule. Depending on whether or not you work during the day, evening or overnights, there are two of you at home and you work split shifts, you work from home, etc., you want to establish your potty schedule and area right from the start.

HOUSE BREAKING

First on the list of things one wants to teach the new puppy/rescue is, generally, potty habits. Establishing good toilet training right from the start will make life immensely easier for everyone concerned. Even older rescues can come with bad house training due to lack of proper training as puppies. They may have been left too many hours in a crate and learned to potty in their crate out of necessity. They may have never learned proper bladder control due to a regular schedule never having been established and maybe even having developed several UTI's, (urinary tract infections), along the way. There are several methods for potty training puppies, but Ian Dunbar introduced the "error proof" method years ago. The basis behind this method is simple, don't allow the puppy to make any mistakes in the house and they will never make any mistakes in the house. I know this "sounds" simple, but there are several ways to accomplish this. For those that work during the day and or any shift longer than a puppy is capable of holding their bladder, offering a potty area indoors for the puppy is a must. The basic rule of thumb for puppies is that they can only "hold it" for as many hours as they are months old. The truth is that the sphincter muscle that controls the bladder is not even developed until the puppy is approximately 4 months old, for some even older. If a puppy wanted to "hold it", they couldn't as they wouldn't have the physical ability to do so. How the indoor potty works is that you set up the crate for the puppy, but attach an xpen to it. Put the puppy's bed in the crate and put the puppy's water and potty area in the xpen. If the only surface you have for the xpen/potty area is carpet, I recommend getting some of the thicker linoleum and putting it over the carpet. Linoleum scraps are not too expensive and they will save your carpet. Whether you decide to use a potty box, (the under the bed plastic storage boxes work well for puppies), with shredded paper, shavings or sod, (grass growing over soil-which is best-heavy plastic can be used under sod), you will want to have it over a surface that will not absorb the moisture and ammonia smell from the urine. You will need to clean the potty area often and encourage the puppy to go outside as much as possible when you ARE home. For the adult or larger rescue, this may seem a bit prohibitive, but trying to work something out for the benefit of the rescue, knowing that it is short term will be well worth the effort. What needs to be understood is that the rescue is NOT the one at fault for his/her lack of house training, some stupid human did not do their job somewhere along the way and now the rescue has been left to suffer. It is now your job, and you are supposed to be the intelligent thinking one, to fix what someone else could not. The 4 P's will be your best friend. They should become your mantra when "potty training" your puppy/rescue.

When you are home, or for those that can be home during the day, the umbilical cord approach can be used. Simply attach the puppy or rescue to you by a 6' leash. This keeps the puppy/rescue within eye shot at all times. You will know when they are awake and when they are asleep. The minute they awaken and start to sniff for a place to potty you will be right there to rush them out to the potty area. Keep a schedule of what happens and when. Fill in when they sleep, when they potty, when they have a bowel movement, what times you are feeding them, when they are active and playful, etc. This will let you know what schedule they are on, so that when you detach them from you, you will be able to predict what time you will be able to take them out before they need to go, thus preventing an accident. Prevention is truly the best medicine when working toward house breaking a puppy/rescue. Each time there is an incident, the odor and habit of going in the incorrect place is instilled and you will have to work harder to train the rescue/puppy to go in the proper place.

I had one Dane returned to me, one I placed against my better judgment. She was a little over a year old when she was returned. She was not leash trained, could not be bathed, have her nails trimmed had no recall-in that she did not know her name, which I changed, and she was not house trained. I came to find out she had been crated all day long, some days someone had come to let her out at noon to potty, some days not. When her owners got home they shoved her out of the crate and into the back yard, then back into the crate. Because she was "unmanageable"-untrained-they resorted to a prong collar and abused her with the prong collar.

In self-defense she turned to putting her mouth on the arm of the abuser-no biting, thanks to good bite inhibition on my part as a puppy, but she was warning, she was tired of getting hurt. She came back to me one really messed up rescue, un-socialized, high energy and untrained, with the exception that as a puppy she had learned that if she pitched a fit she did not have to do what she did not want to. Fortunately she came back to me and she and I quickly had a meeting of the minds. Getting to run on the farm was a big plus for her, but gaining an understanding that you don't get to tell the humans "no" was a lesson she had to learn in order to become a good companion. The hardest problem to fix with her was the house training. She had been urinating in her crate for so long, even though we had a regular schedule and she went out 4 times a day, I worked an overnight shift, so was home during the day, she would still potty right at the front door of her cubby. (She was in a 6' X 8' area that was 4' high chain link so she did not have to be in a crate. These are the cubbies I use for all my rescues/re-homes now.) It took longer for her than any other rescue I have ever worked with, but she finally got it. It took many extra potty outings, just so she would know she was going to go out, staying outside with her to ensure she was going when she was outside and lots of praise when she did go outside. It was heart breaking seeing what she had to go through, all because I didn't listen to my own instincts when I didn't feel this puppy was the right match for that family even though they insisted they wanted this puppy. She paid the price for my hard lesson learned.

Rewarding the rescue/puppy for going in the proper place is important. Everything you can do to help your new companion understand that going outside to potty is preferable to going anywhere else is your goal. Using both verbal and physical praise as well as food treats as rewards for going potty outside, on leash on command and in the designated potty area will soon have your puppy/rescue successfully house trained.

If you do have a puppy or older rescue that seems to be really having a harder time with the training, try taking them out more often and giving them 5 cookies or using some special cookie for the potty cookie, one that they really like. Be patient and remember-this is one of my favorite sayings when mothers were all sitting around talking about the ages of their children and whether or not they were "house broken" yet, "Don't worry too much, they'll all be house broken by the time they go to college." My daughter used to get really mad at me when I would talk about peoples' children and refer to it as "house breaking", but you get the idea. Persistence, patience and praise are the keys.

You have the option of the crate xpen set up, or the umbilical cord set up. You can also train to a bell on the door. Your puppy/rescue has to be aware that they need to go out in order to start implementing this game plan; however, you can start training the basic elements necessary for it to work much earlier.

The first step is to teach the puppy/rescue to "touch". You want them to take their paw and touch your hand initially. If they are very small you can teach them to use their nose. Put a food treat in your hand and give the command "touch". Your puppy/rescue will most likely offer several behaviors in an effort to try to get the treat. When they offer the one you want for them to ring the bell on the door, give them the treat.

Once they are offering the behavior when you give the command without offering others first, in other words, they have figured out which behavior gets the treat when they hear the word "touch", continue without the treat in your hand. You will give the command, "touch" but instead of the treat being in the hand you want them to touch, you will hold it out of sight in the other hand and give the treat after they have given you the behavior once you have given the command.

When they will touch your hand without the treat in it, on command, you are ready to go to the bell on the door. Give the command, "touch". This time point to the bell. When they touch the bell, give them the treat. Repeat this step several times. Continue with this step until you feel they are consistently ringing the bell when you give the command, "touch". The next step is to have them touch the bell and take them outside. Repeat this several times. They will not equate going outside with going potty just yet, but they will start to put ringing the bell together with going outside.

Now that they have an understanding of ringing the bell to go outside, each time before you take them outside to go potty, have them touch the bell. (One of the reasons I suggest waiting a little later to start this training is because if you have a puppy that does not have good bladder control, trying to get them to ring the bell, when they are needing to be rushed out the door before having an "accident" is just asking for trouble.) It will still take some time before the light bulb goes on for them to realize that they can initiate you opening the door to let them out by ringing the bell on their own. Many times they will go through a phase, once they do figure this out, where they will ring the bell for no reason what so ever, just to be let out. You will need to ride out this storm and keep letting them out, regardless of how often they ring the bell. This too shall pass, but if you do not consistently do your job while they are learning theirs, they will not continue to consistently ring the bell when the "need" arises.

POTTY AREA

You will want to establish a potty area in your yard as soon as you bring your new companion home. This should be an area that you have chosen before you bring the puppy/rescue home. You want to take the puppy/rescue to the area, give your command to "go potty" and stand like a statue so that you do not distract the puppy/rescue. If the area is fenced you can start with them off leash, but if it is not, they will need to be on leash. I train all my puppies to go potty on leash on command and start all rescues doing this as well. Some adult rescues will be very intimidated about going potty with a human in close proximity. If this seems to be the case with your new companion, allow them the needed space in the beginning, but after the first week, get a long line or flexi and start asking them to go potty on lead, on command. Start with the morning potty, when they will have the fullest bladder and need to go the worst, thus they will feel the least "inhibited" by your presence. Give them as much room as possible, stand as quietly as possible. Once they go potty, praise them and give them three cookies. It won't be long before they will become comfortable with your presence and potty on leash on command.

It can be easy to get frustrated with this process if you have a puppy/rescue that is easily distracted. Any movement from you, leaves falling from trees, passing butterflies, can, at times, be enough to distract some puppies/rescues mid squat and leave you standing and waiting in the cold, wet, and nastiest of weather. Patience is necessary to get the job done.

ESTABLISHING THE YARD

When I first started taking in rescues, my main concern was keeping them on the property. Although the majority of the area was fenced, the driveway was not gated. My Danes had all been trained not to pass a designated imaginary line, but these new rescues had no idea where that line was, nor did they know what my property was, or that they were not to go over to the house area. I brought all the rescues into the barn area, the office and tack areas were heated and air conditioned and the rescues could also stay in empty horse stalls during the day. I wanted them to be able to run around and get exercise when I was at the barn, but did not trust that as they did not know me and I did not know them, that they would not run off. My solution to the problem was to attach them to a lunge line and allowed them to run around at the end of it with me while I went around the barn area doing chores. I did this for two weeks, what I consider to be the adjustment period, doing short recalls while I had them on the lunge line, to ensure they had a recall and that they knew their name.

One of the surprise advantages I found to this rather long umbilical cord approach was that after two weeks staying within the same perimeter, once the lunge line was removed, the rescues all stayed within the area that had been established during the first two weeks.

What you will want to do, for the first two weeks, every time you go out into your yard with your rescue/puppy is to have them on a long line, at least 30' long. Go about your business walking around the perimeter of your yard. Allow your puppy/rescue to tag along, investigating whatever they want along the way. Make sure they stay inside your "yard". If they are a short distance away and turn to run toward you, once they are committed, use their name and come. Give them a few cookies and tons of praise when they arrive. These are not formal recalls; you are just setting the framework for later recalls. You are establishing that getting to you gets praise and a food reward. Many rescues will have difficulty with recalls. Many times rescues will have come from situations where they were crated or tied out for far too long and when given the sweet taste of freedom, being the intelligent creatures they are, had no desire to return to their previous incarceration. What followed was then an unpleasant chase, getting caught, which was followed by an inappropriate negative response by the human. Of course each time this situation repeated itself it just got worse for all concerned, thus developing a recall issue for the rescue. In order to reverse this, you have to make coming a positive experience and this starts on the long line with the rescue coming voluntarily and leaving again because they choose to. After two weeks of positively reinforcing the voluntary recall, you will have set the stage for the next phase of recall work over the next few weeks.

One other important note here, some rescues have had such a negative experience, and have attached such a negative connotation to the word "come" that I have had their new owners change the command. But for now, the recall is not formal and we are doing this on leash, so if you see that "come" is an issue for your rescue, change the word.

WHO AM I?

Whether you have a new puppy or you are bringing home a rescue, there is a good chance the name given to this precious being will be new. I had a re-home that had been with his family for close to a year. I had gotten a card at Christmas with a picture and all looked well. Less than 6 months later I got a call that there might be an ad in the paper that someone was trying to give away a Dane. They thought the phone number was familiar. By the time I got the number and called them they had given the dog away-even though it states in my contract the dog HAS to come back to me, but these people didn't bother or care. Fortunately, I suppose, the people that took the dog also got the puppy book that I send with all the puppies I place and found my number and called me, as they felt I was a breeder that cared about my Danes. He was unhealthy and needed care. I offered to take him back until he was well and return him to this family if they still wanted him. They felt they could care for him and chose to keep him and care for him themselves, against my better judgment, I agreed to allow them to do so. A few weeks later I got a call asking me to take him back. Of course I would. I picked up a horribly emaciated excuse for a Dane. I was mortified. He was in the back of the vehicle in a Doberman sized crate in a puddle of urine without even so much as a blanket to soak it up. I carried him to my van and went straight to my vet. The original owners told the people I picked him up from, that he had fungal pneumonia-and that they couldn't get him to take the pills. The people I got him from told me he wouldn't eat, take meds, etc. My vet tested for a number of things, all of which came up negative. We determined that his only issue was severe malnutrition, to the point that he had neurological deficiencies. That is severe malnutrition! The point of this story is, I changed his name, he was starting over when he came back to me, and he needed a new name for his new start. I renamed him Justin, after the boots-they are sturdy and strong and last a very, very, very long time. I nursed him back to health, wondering what issues he had that led his family to neglect him so-he had none. Even in his condition he did not want to potty inside, he did not bark, he got along with all the other dogs and still loved all people. I could not figure out for the life of me why anyone would do what they did to this dog, but there it was. There is a happy ending to this story; he was re-homed with a wonderful young woman that gave him the home, life and love he deserved. I only wish he hadn't had to go through such hell in the interim.

Okay, so back on point, he had a new name and needed to learn to respond to his new name. As opposed to some households with only one puppy/rescue, so only one name and one to respond to said name, I generally have numerous Danes that are willing to respond at any given time. Getting each to recognize and respond to their name is important. I start by sitting next to each one and quietly calling their name. When they turn their head toward me, I will reward them with a cookie. Once they are responding to their name when I am sitting next to them by turning their heads I will sit a little farther away and repeat the process. I like to "jack pot", or give multiple cookies for any movement toward me. Through this process the puppy/rescue learns that this "name" has significance for them and that looking to you and moving toward you will get them a reward.

FIRST TWO WEEKS IN REVIEW

1. Fill your pocket with cookies.
2. Learn the 4 P's of positive puppy training.
3. Establish a routine.
4. Establish the rules.
5. Catch them doing something right.
6. House breaking.
7. Establishing a potty area.
8. Establishing a yard.
9. Informal recalls.
10. Familiarizing them with their name.

Although these items are in order, you will be introducing them-clearly-nearly simultaneously. The first two weeks that you have your puppy/rescue in your home are vital to establishing the basis of your new relationship. As much as I know that it is not possible for most of us to take 2 weeks off to spend this time with our new companions to get them settled in, spending as much time as we do have will go a long way to helping them feel that this is their new home, a permanent home, that they are not just a guest so that they can start bonding with you and the two of you can start building your new relationship together.

CHAPTER THREE

BASIC OBEDIENCE

Basic obedience with puppies is all fun and games; however, there is still structure. First your puppy/rescue needs to know that you are working, unlike before where you were just rewarding them because you "caught them doing something right", now you will be going to be asking for something specific and rewarding for something specific. You will need attention in order for them to learn anything and you are going to have to pay attention in order to know if they are getting it right. This training game is a two way street. To establish that a training session is about to begin, I use a phrase to indicate that this is what is about to happen. You can come up with your own, I use, "Let's go to work." Any time during the training session that I feel I need to remind my puppy/rescue and later adult that we are not finished and we are still in a training session I can use the word "working" as a reminder. So whatever phrase you choose, make sure there is a word that you can repeat as a reminder when necessary, for example, I use "working".

You will need a one word release word for between exercises. I use the word "free". This is a word that you will use frequently. When you are teaching positional commands, one position at a time, sit, down, stand, etc., you will use the release command after each one to allow the puppy/rescue to move out of position, after you have given them the treat, release them, then you can praise and play with them. Although the treat, release, praise and play all happen nearly simultaneously, the release command, "free", or whatever you decide to use, is important to allow your puppy/rescue out of position so that they can get up and play with you.

Finally you need an end of training session phrase. I use "All done." Again, use whatever you like, but use a different word than what you use for your beginning of training session command.

Once you give the beginning of training session command, be committed to giving 100% of your attention to the training session and expect the same from your companion. When you first start working with your companion, keep your training sessions short, no more than 5-10 minutes. As your companion learns more and grows older you can lengthen the sessions. Always end the sessions before your companion gets bored. You want to end the sessions when you feel your companion is still looking for more. In this way they will be looking forward to the next session.

You will generally want to start your session with training that involves movement. This will get your companion engaged with you and interacting with you. You can then move on to stationary commands and finish up with movement again.

I like to start off lead in a safe area, either a basement, large living room or small fenced in area. I want to be able to get my companions attention, but I don't want them to be able to get distracted or to be able to wonder off.

GET IN

Get in, as in "get in heel position". This is the precursor to any heeling. We all want to be able to take our companions out for a walk, on leash and not be pulled along like we are water skiing. The first step in this process is to get our companions into the correct position. With the cookie in your left hand, face your companion. Put the cookie in front of your companion's nose and draw them toward your left side. As you are doing this, step backwards. Continue to draw your companion backwards until they pass your side. Now turn them toward you and bring them forward as you step forward and bring their nose up past your leg and treat them when their head is past your leg. Give your release command. Praise and play with your companion. Repeat this process about 10 times. You will want to start saying, "get in", as you treat your companion, as they are in the correct position. Be sure that you do not treat them too soon-when they are too far back. You do not want them to get the idea that "heel" position is behind you. You want to be sure that they get the treat when their head is in front of your leg.

You want them to start to get the idea that "get in" has some meaning before you progress, so I will repeat this part of the exercise for at least a week before I add any heeling steps.

As their training progresses, as you feel your companion has an understanding of what "get in" means, you can give the command earlier-still using the food treat as a lure to help them find the correct position-but you will be taking fewer steps backward and forward by this time. The next step in the training process would be to be able to give the command "get in" and have your companion come to heel position by your left side, ready for your next request.

WALKING IN HEEL POSITION

If your companion can walk in heel position without a leash, adding the leash will not be an issue. One of the most common problems people make is putting a leash on the animal, the animal pulls, they lean, the animal pulls, they lean and so on. If your companion does not have anything to lean on, if they learn to walk beside you voluntarily they will never BE a leash puller. If they have already established the habit of pulling on the leash, teaching them to "get in" heel position, and to heel without the leash will help to extinguish that behavior.

Ask your companion to "get in". With a treat closely in front of their nose, walk forward two or three steps. Treat, release, praise and play with your companion. I will abbreviate this now to TRPP-treat, release, praise, play. It is important to only go two or three steps and release your companion. I doubt they will stay in position for more than that and you want to reward them-remember the "catch them doing something right" mantra-while they are still correct. Once they are out of position, it is too late and you have missed the opportunity to TRPP. For the next week you will only ask for two to three steps before you TRPP. I know this does not seem like much, but rewarding them for being correct is what is important, not the distance that you go.

After the first week, you should be able to ask for more steps, 5-8 steps before you TRPP. Each week you can continue to build on this. Be careful not to ask for too much too soon. If your companion is getting out of position, just back up and progress more slowly. If you have a very small companion it can be helpful to use a curb or retaining wall in the beginning to save your back. All the bending over can be very hard on your back and you need to have the food treat right in front of your companion's nose or you will not be successful. You can also use a wooden dowel or spoon and use squeeze cheese or peanut butter on the end.

The key to success is slow progression. Do not ask for more than your companion can do. TRPP before your dog is out of position. Once you have mastered 10-15 steps in a straight line, start to move in a gradual curve to the right or left. Progress from this gradual curve in one direction to serpentines. Once you master serpentines, you can start to add distractions; small toys or treats on the ground, on chairs, a child going past on a bike, a ball rolling past, etc. You want to work on all of these things at home, in a controlled environment BEFORE taking your puppy/rescue out into the real world and expecting them to be able to focus on you. This is not to say you will not be taking them out for walks, socializing them and having them on leash, just don't expect a perfectly well behaved heeling companion and don't punish them for not doing perfectly and well what they are only just now learning.

STATIONARY EXERCISES

SIT

For the sit, again, I do not have my companion on leash, but I will have a flat buckle collar on them during training sessions. With your companion in front of you, put the finger of your right hand in the collar on the underside of the neck.

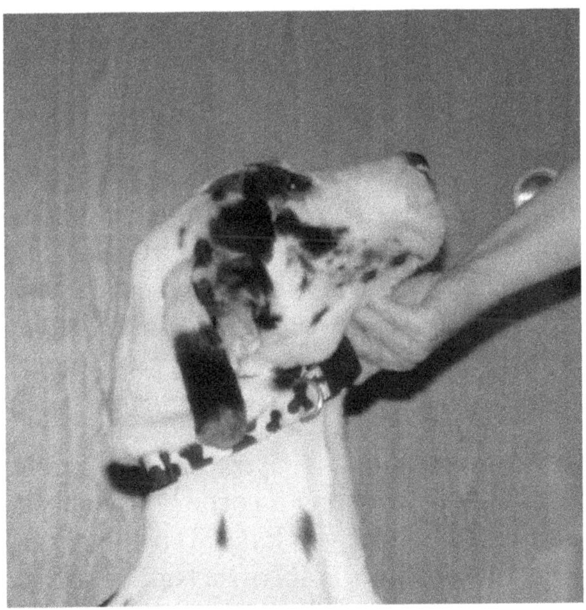

Tolkien has already started to sit. Mary has her finger gently under his chin, under the collar. Don't let the excess skin fool you, Mary is using a very light pressure, Tolkien just has a lot of loose skin!

With the food treat in your left hand, palm facing up, bring the treat directly over your companion's nose. Put a slight pressure on the collar forward and up as you hold the treat over your companion's nose. The theory here is that your companion will want to work against the pressure; if the pressure is forward and up, and the cookie is directly over their nose, the butt is going to go down. As soon as the rear hits the floor, TRPP.

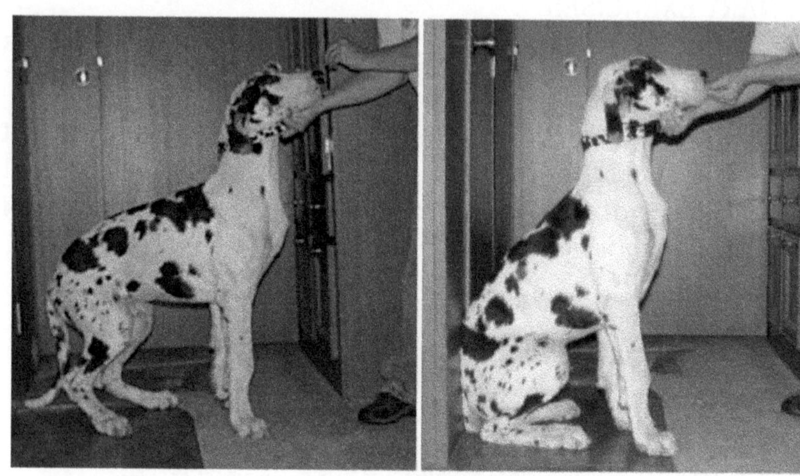

Mary has the treat in the proper position, but she is making a common mistake with her left hand. She has her palm facing down instead of up. She has corrected this in the second photo. You want the position of your hand to be consistent with the signal you will use later. Mary is giving Tolkien the cookie as soon as his rear hits the floor. She is using a corner to keep him from backing up.

Repeat the process 10 times. If you have a problem with your companion backing up, try using a corner. If you are still having a problem, try adjusting where you have your finger under the collar, generally I find the position is incorrect-off to the side instead of going directly up under the chin. Another common mistake is to hold the treat too far above the nose. Be sure to use the release command as soon as you give the treat, as soon as the butt hits the floor. Timing is everything.

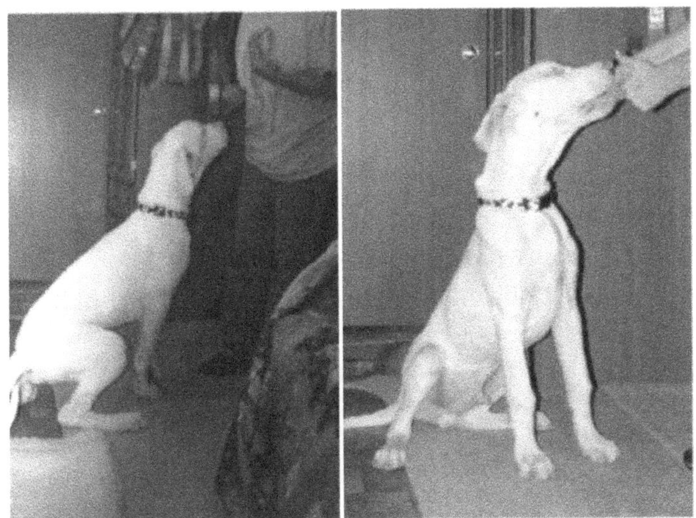

Wizard is a deaf puppy. He has learned the hand signal for sit. He is given the reward, as well as the sign for "good boy", a thumbs up.

Timing **is** everything. You want to be sure that you give the treat the minute the rear hits the floor. Release, praise and play with your companion to let them know they have just done a wonderful thing. Adding the word "sit" can come as soon as they are starting to sit when you present the treat. In the beginning they are only sitting because of the food lure, so once the lure is working to get them to sit, you can start to add the command to start to make the association with the position.

Once you start adding the command, be sure to only give it once. If you repeat the command multiple times they will begin to wait for the final command-"sit, sit, sit", becomes the command, instead of "sit"-before they respond. Don't allow yourself to get caught in this trap. Give the command once and give your companion time to respond. TRPP.

As your companion becomes more responsive with the command you can begin to delay, by only a second or two, the release command. You will be beginning to set the stage for the wait and stay commands that you will be using later-much later. You do want to be sure that you do not over do this. In other words, do not push this process. If your companion starts to break before you release them you will start to set a bad precedent. There are going to be many times when you are going to need your companion to stay or wait in one of the stationary positions and teaching a solid stay and wait are going to be important. Making sure you always release them before they break now will help to prevent future mistakes and will make later training easy.

You may not think these things are important now, so I will give you a few examples; when going to the vet, your companion will need to do a stand stay for the exam, vaccinations, etc., while waiting to go through a doorway or out of the vehicle door, they may need to wait until it is safe, if you have guests over and need for them to stay while they come in and not run out the door, if you have a child eating at the table and you don't want them to swipe their food from their hand or plate you may want them to stay out of a room or down stay until the child is finished eating. These are just a few examples, but as daily life goes on you will find many more. Although I am stressing the importance of learning stay and wait, these are not things you will be teaching now, only setting the stage for. Until your companion truly knows the stationary exercises, they cannot be expected to understand that they are to "stay" in any position. I feel my companion has a true understanding of the stationary exercises when I can give the command and or signal and they quickly respond and give the correct response without the aid of a treat. If they will do this 10 out of 10 times, they are ready to start learning stay. Until they pass this test I do not start training stays. One of the reasons is that I do not use food at all when training stays. Food encourages movement and movement is the one thing I don't want when I am training stays.

DOWN

Many companions are uncomfortable with the down position. This is a submissive position. For this reason you do not want to force your companion into the down. You want to encourage them into this position on their own. There are several ways to do this. Start with your companion in the sit position. If you have difficulty with their rear popping up, you can either place their rear near a corner or wall or place your left hand on their rear to keep them from getting up, put the treat in your right hand and bring it toward their nose and in toward their chest. From there, draw their nose in and down to the floor and then draw it along the floor.

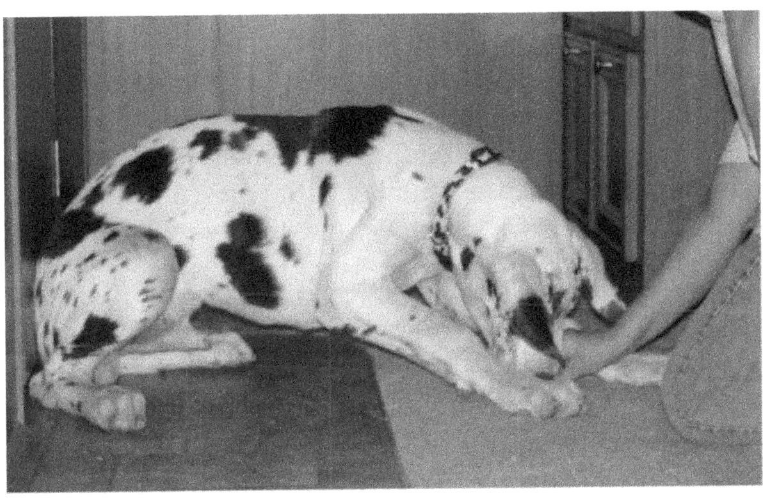

Mary is using a wall to help keep Tolkien's rear down as he goes into the down. This is very nice positioning of the treat to "walk" his front into the down.

You may need to help "walk" their front feet forward the first few times. Give them the cookie as soon as their elbows are on the floor.

If this method just isn't working, you can try this alternative. Sit on the floor with one knee bent. Your companion can be standing or sitting. Bring the treat under your knee and put it in front of your companion's nose. Draw your companion under your knee with the treat. They will have to crawl to get under your knee. As soon as they get their elbows on the floor, help them get their rear on the floor as well. It shouldn't take much and they generally have their rear there already. Just as with the sit, once they have the idea with the lure, start to add the command, "down". Remember to TRPP asap.

As you progress with sit and down, you can encourage your puppy to remain in position longer by quietly praising them while you gently and slowly stroke them. Do this for only a few more seconds before you release and play with them. You will have given them the treat as soon as they were in position and were quietly praising them, both verbally and physically with the gentle, slow stroking. You will have asked them to remain in position for a few seconds and THEN release and play with your companion. It is still too early to begin work on stays, but they can learn to hold the position while you praise them.

Some trainers like to start to ask for the down from the stand sooner than later. I tend to wait until later. If you are working with a large breed puppy, there tends to be a delay in the development between the neuro-transmitters that connect the front and rear ends before they are 5 or 6 months of age. Trying to get them to go into a down from a stand is nearly impossible since the "connection" isn't quite there. Smaller breeds mature faster and do not tend to have this issue.

STAND

You will need to start with your companion in the sit position. Put your right finger in the collar and the treat between two fingers on your left hand. As you are standing with your companion on your left, move your left hand, palm facing your companion, across in front of the nose of your companion. Give the command "stand" as they follow the food lure. Take a slight step forward if you need to, to get your companion to stand up. As soon as they are standing, give them the treat, and move your left hand back toward their belly area. This is so that if they try to sit you can catch them. The finger in their collar is to prevent them walking off once they are standing. TRPP. You will want to repeat this process 10 times. The idea is to get them into the stand and to have them stand still. Be sure to release them as soon as you have the stand and they are still, but not to ask for this for more than a second or two. They will start to wiggle and move about very quickly, so remember not to ask for too much too soon.

CHAINING COMMANDS

Your companion will begin to understand the individual commands for sit, down and stand. They will still need the food lure, and you will most likely need to keep your hands on them, stroking them, to keep them in position until you release them. Once you see that they are responding to the verbal command, they are ready for you to start chaining the commands. Chaining is simply putting more than one command together. You will start by asking for only two positions at a time. For example, you would ask for the sit, then down, then TRPP. You might ask for the sit, then stand and TRPP. You can go from the stand to the down and TRPP. You want to start with chaining no more than two commands at a time.

Your companion will begin to understand the chaining of two commands at which time you can move ahead to three. Once they are proficient at three, you can move ahead to four. Once you get to four, you can vary the number that you chain before you TRPP. It becomes a game between you and your companion. They will learn to go from position to position faster and faster to get the treat at the end and to play with and be praised by you.

RECALL

Earlier we worked to gain name recognition. This is the very first step in getting a good solid recall and should be well established after two weeks of working on this. You worked on recalls when you had your companion on the long line. You will have established whether or not the word come is an issue for this particular individual. If "come" is on their list of nasty four letter words, you will need to use a different word for recalls.

Now that your recall work is more formal, this is the time to have your companion on leash. You want them to understand that when they hear their name and come that no is not an option. What you need to understand is that your job is to make recalls fun. When your companion gets to you, it should always end in a party.

Start facing your companion. Move away-dogs are more likely to move toward movement, as opposed to a stationary object. As your companion starts to move toward you, use their name and "come" and as soon as they reach you, TRPP. You can give them a food treat, whip out a favorite toy to play with, toss a toy for them to play with but don't allow them to run off with it, keep them close and encourage them to bring it to you to play with them.

Repeat this process 10 times. Each time you want to have a party with your companion when they reach you. If at any time they are slow to respond, decide they are more interested in something else or start to veer off before they get to you, give a mild/gentle tug on the leash and use your voice and or the toy to encourage them to come to you. Remember to keep moving. Don't stand still until they get to you. You need to remain very animated during recall work.

As your companion becomes more reliable, use a longer line, but keep your companion attached to you. My rule of thumb is that until I am willing to bet someone $50 that my companion will come when I call, I do not practice recalls without the long line. There are several more steps to go through before you will be ready to call your companion and know they will be reliable, but it will come. This does not mean that you cannot call your companion when you want them, just do not use their name and "come". For example, if you have taken them out to potty and they have had some play time and now it is time for breakfast, run to the door and call their name and call them for breakfast. "Yoo-hoo, breakfast!" Once they are committed, only a few feet from you, then you can praise them and use the word come, just as you did previously for the voluntary recalls.

A reliable recall is vital to a happy partnership. There is nothing more frustrating than being in a situation where you need your companion to come and they just won't, or worse, they let you get within a few feet and then take off again. It always reminds me of a pony my father used to own. The pony would race home from putting the cattle in the field, hell bent for leather and then for no good reason put on the brakes. My father would go flying over his head. The pony would then proceed past him, heading for home and stop about 20' away. He would wait until my father was about 5' from him and take off again, another 20'. This process repeated itself until they made it back to the farm. My father was, of course, by this time hopping mad and was never going to get the pony caught. My grandfather would get him caught and unsaddled and send my father into the house to clean up. You don't want your companion to develop this habit. To ensure that this doesn't happen, keep the work fun, always have a party when they arrive and don't take them off leash too soon.

HEELING RECALL

This is the second step in working on recalls. Because you are working on recalls you will start this exercise on leash. When you feel your companion is fairly reliable, has a good understanding of the word come and knows that getting to you is going to be a positive experience, it is time to start heeling recalls. Ask your companion to "get in", and follow this with a short bit of heeling. By this time your companion should be heeling for 10 steps or so. At this point call your companion's name and "come" and start running backwards. When your companion gets to you, TRPP. You will always be facing forward, never changing direction. Your companion will be the one that changes direction and turns toward <u>you</u>, then runs toward <u>you</u>. The majority of the time, when you call your companion, they will be looking and or moving away from you, their attention will be on something that is anything other than you. When you call their name, you want them to turn toward you and look at you and as soon as you call to them to "come" you want them to come running toward you as fast as they can. By starting with the heeling recalls you are actually starting to "pattern" the behavior you want. This is why it is important that you are facing forward and run backwards and that you use their name and "come" AND that your companion is the one that turns toward you and runs to you. As per usual you will TRPP as soon as they arrive. When you and your companion are successfully executing the heeling recalls on a 6' leash, take them off leash. Remember that you are doing this from the heel-they are at your side, not a distance from you. If at any time there are any issues with them hesitating to come, put the leash back on and go back to working at the shorter distance for a short time and then try again. Working without the 6' leash will allow you to run backwards faster and get a little more distance between the two of you for the recall. This should build drive and bring your companion in even faster.

You will continue your recall work with either one or two people, if you have access to a helper. You will use a long line for this type of recall work. Run the long line out the distance you will be moving away from your companion so that should you see any signs of hesitation you have it available to assist you to "reel your companion in".

Using a helper, have them restrain your companion as you show them a toy and walk 5 feet away. You will want to encourage them to look at you and tease them a bit as you walk away, but be sure that you stay facing them. When you are approximately 5' from them, call your companions name and "come", your assistant can let them go, at which time you will run away from your companion for the next 5' and when they catch up to you-TRPP. If you don't have a person to help you, you can put a large ring into a wall, a large ring into the ground and run a long line through it or run a long line around a post, attach one end to your companions collar and hold the other end yourself such that you are the one actually restraining your own puppy/rescue until you call them to come to you.

When you have a fast recall at 10', wait until you are 10' away to call them and run until you reach 20'. When they are proficient at 20', progress to 30'.

Once your companion is doing a good fast recall at 30', you can add a distraction at the ½ way point. Use a small treat, something not nearly as good as what they will get when they get to you, or a small toy. Make sure you have a long line attached when you start adding the distraction. You want your companion to be running so fast toward you that they don't even notice the distraction, but if they do, you will have the long line attached and if they hesitate at all at the distraction, you can give them a gentle tug and encourage them to come on in to you. Praise them lavishly when they get to you. If they did not notice the distraction, give them a big jackpot-several cookies, if they noticed the distraction, but came running in with a little assistance, still jackpot. You want them to know that getting to you is the best reward ever! You want to remind them that getting to you, when you call them to come will always be worth it.

STAY/WAIT

Stay means stay and wait means wait. What I mean is, when I tell a dog to stay, I mean until I return to you and release you, it is until farther notice, do not move. When I use the command wait, it means I want you to pay attention, there is another command coming. Wait is a short term command and I will most likely release my dog to go somewhere or do something without returning to them first. Why do I make this distinction? Some dogs need it. Some dogs are so intelligent that the concept of stay, once learned means exactly that and if you want them to move or do anything else, you had better use another word. Some dogs don't care and this distinction isn't necessary. Because I don't know which one I may have when I start, I teach both.

I wait to teach stay until I know the positional commands are understood. This is to say, if I say or signal the sit, I will get a sit immediately. I do not have to use a food lure to get the sit. If I signal or say down, I will get a down. I need to know that my companion is reliable on the stationary positions before I start stays. If they do not KNOW the positions and cannot get into them without a food lure, how can I expect them to understand that I want them to stay in that position?

Wait is a little different. Because I am not asking them to hold the position for a long period of time, I will start using wait earlier in the training process. I can keep my hands on my companion most of the time while I am using wait, before I give the release command. For this reason, we will start with wait.

There are many situations in which you can use the wait command; if you want to go through the door first and release your companion to come through behind you, if you want them to wait to come out of the car door until you get the leash attached to their collar, if you are walking them and you accidently drop the leash and you want them to wait a second while you pick up the leash, if you need to get through a narrow place and you want to get through first and then call them through after you. These are just a few examples, but in everyday life, there will be many.

To start teaching wait, and you have already started by using your release command and delaying the use of it to have your companion hold the position just a bit longer. A doorway is the easiest place to start to give them the idea of what you want. Sit your companion on the inside of the doorway. They are used to waiting to hear the release command. Now you will add a hand signal and "wait" after you give the positional command. The hand signal is your palm, fingers together, facing your companion's nose. Bring your hand, like a stop sign in front of their nose. As you do this, give the verbal command "wait". Step away from your companion on the leg that is away from your companion, in other words step away on the right leg. The first time you do this, keep your hand on your companion, just to ensure that they do not move until you give the release command. Step through the doorway, give the release command, "free", and allow your companion to come to you. When they come to you through the door, proceed forward 4 or 5 steps in heel position, release again and TRPP. The reason you want to heel forward a few steps before you praise and play with your companion is to discourage them from "breaking", thinking they are entirely off the hook because they are outside and can run off. As they gain confidence, lengthen the amount of time before you release them to come through the door. The key to success is not to ask for too much too soon. Keep your hand on them and stay close until you feel that they are comfortable remaining in place until you release them. At that point you are ready to give the wait command and step away without having to have a hand on them. From there, you can gradually lengthen the amount of time that you ask them to remain in place before you release them. I am only talking about 5 seconds here. When you feel your companion is proficient with the doorway, add other locations. Try getting out of the car and training the wait command. If your companion anticipates when the door is opened, you can have someone on the other side of the car holding their leash to prevent them from coming out of the car until you give the release command. Any time you find a situation that the wait command will come in handy, set the situation up, and train for it.

Stay is a little more complex. I will give you the beginning steps here, but for a complete understanding and training guide for stays, when you feel you need them, I would recommend my book Rock Solid Stays.

As previously stated, your companion must have a complete understanding of the stationary positions. I do not use food when I am training stays. Food encourages movement and movement is the one thing you do not want when you are training stays. The key to success when training stays is prevention of mistakes. You will start by sitting your companion on your left side. Put your right finger in the collar and give the stay signal, just as you did the wait signal with your left hand. Step directly in front of your companion, stepping out with your right leg, the leg that is away from your companion. Keep your hands on your companion, then in a low soothing voice let them know this is a good sit, a good stay. Remain directly in front of your companion for 5 seconds and then step right back into place by their right side. You are going to give the stay signal and command 4 more times. After the 5th time you are going to heel your companion forward, release and play with them. Set them back up where they were before and repeat the entire process. Do the same thing for the down. Depending on how well your companion holds the stand, you can either stay beside them for the first few days-if they are really having trouble holding the stand stay, to ensure they stand and don't try to sit. Once they understand you want them to remain standing, then you can step in front, and continue as with the previous exercises.

Not all dogs are the same. Some will pick up staying in one position faster than the other. Some can hold the stay for 5 seconds in the beginning without any problems; others will have to start with 2 seconds. It doesn't matter what your companion is capable of, it is your job to figure it out and help them be successful.

Once your companion is successful at 5 seconds, increase the time to 10 seconds, then 15 seconds, 20 seconds, 30 seconds, 40 seconds, 50 seconds and finally 1 minute. When they can hold the stay with you directly in front of them for one minute you are ready to add a little distance. You can now step 2' away, BUT you will drop the time back to 5 seconds. You will gradually increase the time to 1 minute as you did before but only as they are successful. When they are successful at 2' and 1 minute, you will increase the distance to 4', then 6', 10', 15', 20', 25', and finally 30'. Remember that every time you increase the distance you will go back to 5 seconds and gradually increase the time again for each of the positions. Eventually you want to get up to 3 minutes on the sit stay, 5 minutes on the down stay and 1 minute on the stand stay.

If at any time during your training you have a problem with your companion breaking, back up, you are trying to progress too quickly. Use your voice to try to catch them if you are working at a distance and cannot get your hands or self to your companion quickly enough to prevent a mistake. You can use a verbal correction, "ungh, ungh". Your voice can travel faster than you can to try to prevent a mistake. Should your companion get out of position, don't make an issue out of it-you are the one that has made the mistake in pushing them too fast. All you need to do is take them back to the spot where they were, reposition them, give the stay command again and then either stay closer and shorten the amount of time you ask them to stay-in other words, back up a few steps in the process.

BASIC OBEDIENCE IN REVIEW

1. Beginning of training session phrase.
2. Release command.
3. End of training session phrase.
4. Get in.
5. Heeling 101.
6. Stationary positional commands-sit/down/stand.
7. Chaining commands.
8. Recall.
9. Heeling recall.
10. Wait.
11. Stay.

The ground work is here for each of these exercises. You should build on what is here as you gain success and confidence and your companion becomes proficient at each step.

CHAPTER FOUR

OBEDIENCE FOR DAILY LIVING

Beyond basic obedience, there are many behaviors that I train that I feel make a companion an asset to live with. These behaviors are mainly ones that are for convenience, but ones that are also very "handy". Some of them also have safety applications.

CLOTHES ON

Whether you have one dog or many, you may or may not want to leave a collar on your companion at all times. I live in the country and my Danes run on several acres. At one time I had collars on them with their tags. I can't tell you how many collars my Danes lost in the fields. I even tried putting hot pink collars on them in hopes of finding the lost collars-no luck. I also felt that with the Danes playing together there was the chance that one might get their mouth caught in another's collar and get injured. For these reasons I chose not to keep collars on my Danes. I teach the behavior "clothes on", which is where they literally put their head into the collar themselves, so that I am not trying to put a collar on a moving target. Even with a collar on your companion, it is always possible for them to slip out of it and or for the collar to break, again, a good reason for them to come running and put their head into a collar held out stretched, or even a leash in a loop, if that is all you have available.

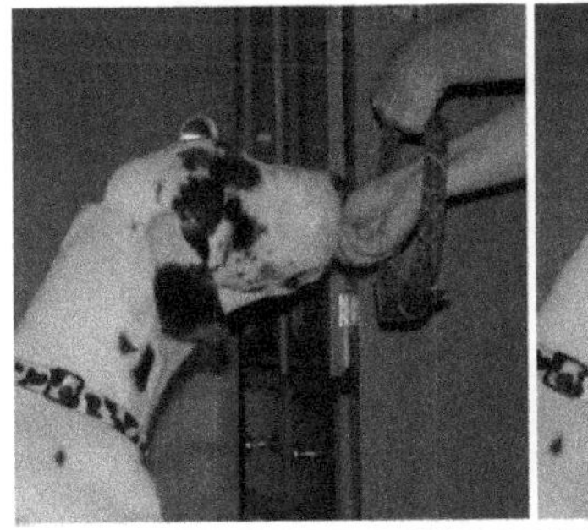
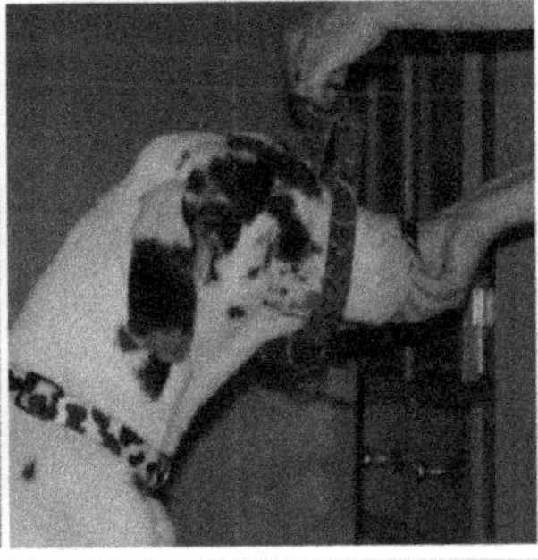

To start teaching this you will need a collar that will be much larger than what they will be wearing so that it will easily slip over their head. With your companion sitting, facing you, slip the collar over your wrist. Put the food treat in your hand and give the command, "clothes on". Give the food treat as you slide the collar over the head and onto their neck. Repeat this step 10 times. Do this for several days. Then you are ready to move on to the next step. Hold the treat at the collar opening, instead of through the collar. Give the command, "clothes on" and slip the collar over your companion's head and onto their neck.

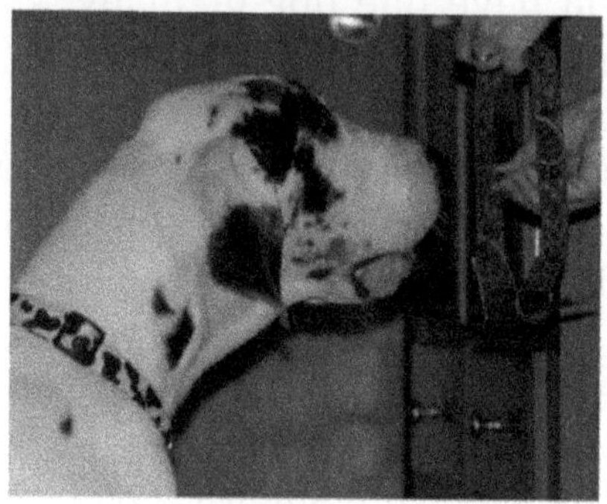

Repeat this step 10 times. As long as they are comfortable with this step, move on to the next step. Hold your hand with the food treat behind the collar, but still in front of your companion's nose.

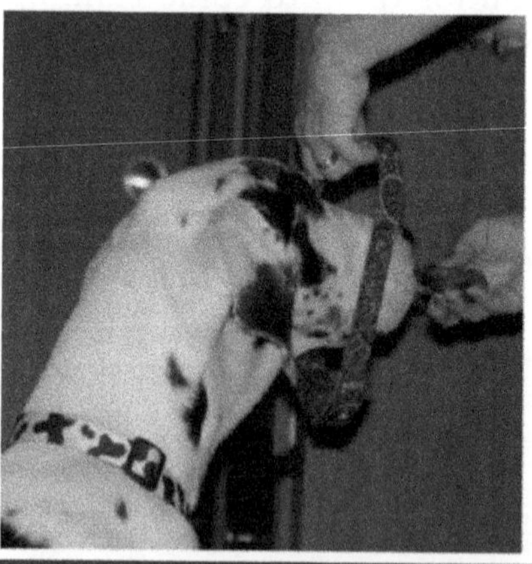

By this time your companion should have a pretty good idea that the collar is to go on their head and that they have to go through the collar to get the treat. Give the command, "clothes on" and wait for them to come through the collar to come after the treat. You can finish putting the collar on them by slipping it on to their neck. With each training session, hold the treat a little farther behind the collar and gradually move the collar farther away from their nose so that they have to get up and move toward the collar to get their head into the collar and on their head to get to the treat. As you continue to progress-and you will want to progress only as they are proficient at each distance-you can start to make a game out of it. You can move away from them as they start to get really good at it. You can stand at an angle to them, you can move it slowly and steadily and make them "work" to get their head in the collar, at which time you would "jack pot" them for accomplishing the task. Keep it fun; make it a game once they know that when the collar is presented, it is their goal to get their head in the collar.

One practical example of when this came in really handy; I was training one of my Danes, a rather large energetic female, Winners, and the class I was to teach was gathering outside the ring. I was nearly finished, I had pumped her up quite a bit as this was necessary to keep her "up" for training, and all of a sudden she slipped out of her collar. I could see that she had zoomie on the brain! All I could think was-not now, not in front of all of my students! I held up her collar and said, "Clothes on". She ran right towards me and put her head right in the collar. I couldn't have been more thrilled for one of my Danes to comply with a command in my whole life. Aside from the fact that it made me look great in front of all of my students-thank you Winners-it was a testament to good training, and a practical application of one of the commands I was stressing in class. You never know when something will happen and you will have a need. I was glad that Winners had that command on her list and that she was well trained and especially in that environment still responsive, even though she was in zoomie mode. THAT is what training is all about!

BEDTIME

There may be times when you have company over and want your companion to be a part of the group, but not in everyone's face. You may be preparing a meal, or eating and there may be small children present. You may be at the vet, visiting a friend or even at a hotel. Any of these situations would be a great place to use the bedtime command.

Start with a blanket or rug that is large enough for your companion to lie down on and stretch out with all of their body on the mat. It is important that it is large enough for all of them to remain on the mat when they stretch out. If you have two people that is great, if not it still works just fine with one. You want to drop a treat on the mat in such a way that your companion does not see you do it. Start about 5' from the mat. Give the command "bedtime". You can pick another word if you like, but be consistent.

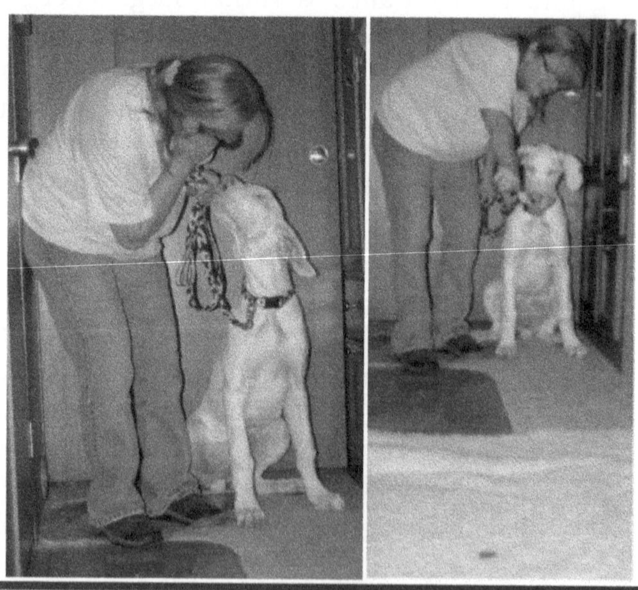

Give the command and take your companion to the mat. Show them the cookie on the mat. Quietly praise them while they are on the mat. Keep them there for about 5 seconds.

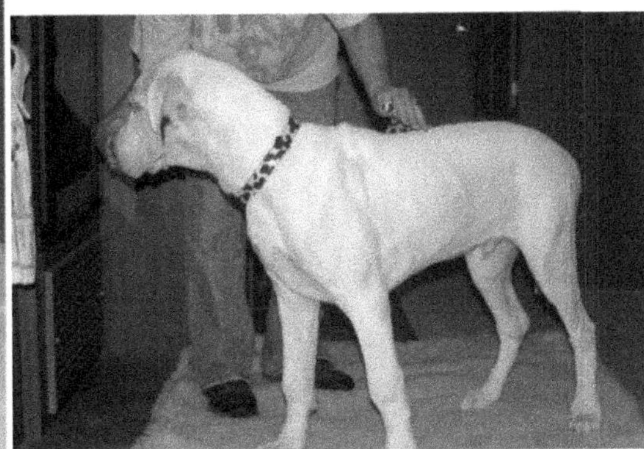

Give the release command "free", and take them off the mat. As you are leaving drop a cookie behind you on the center of the mat.

Because Wizard is deaf, we use hand signals, a lot of food treats and a lot of physical praise. I talk to him even though I know he cannot hear me because it helps me stay focused on what we are doing and keeps my body language and facial expressions consistent. As you can see, he is very attentive-a very good student.

If you have two people, the second person can drop the cookie on the mat as you walk away. Repeat this process 10 times. You will want to do this every day, even several times a day for one week before you progress to the next step.

After the first week you are ready for the next step. Now the cookie is going to come from you instead of being on the mat when they get there. By this time they should be taking you to the mat, expecting to find a cookie there. This is what we want. Give the command, "bedtime" and allow them to get out in front of you if they will. When they get to the mat, give them a cookie. Ask them to sit. Praise them quietly and release them off the mat after 5 seconds. Repeat this several times asking them to stand, or down as well as sit. Once they get the idea, you can ask them to chain two or three positions while they are on the mat before you release them off of the mat.

You want to stay at this stage for another week. When you feel they are going to the mat willingly ahead of you, start to gradually increase the distance that you have them take you to the mat. You do not need to increase the distance more than 15'. You want to be able to send them to the mat, with you following closely behind and have them stay on the mat while you ask them to sit, down, sit, stand, etc., and then release them. As they get the idea, you will increase the amount of time that you ask them to remain on the mat until you release them. It is important that you do not use the words wait or stay. When they are on the bedtime command as much as we want them to remain in one location, we want them to understand that they can change positions as often as possible and get comfortable.

It will take months of practice before you will be able to leave your companion on the mat in the bedtime command for an extended period of time. It is worth spending the time to train this behavior, but it takes time.

ON/OFF SWITCH

Any time you have a behavior you want to get rid of, you need an on/off switch. For example, if your dog barks, I would make the on switch "talk" and the off switch "quiet". If my companion had a bad habit of jumping up on people I would make the on switch "hugs" and the off switch "off", or "feet".

You want to set your companion up to give you the behavior you want to stop. Give them the on switch, and the behavior starts-you know it will because you have set them up. If it is jumping up, for example, you see them coming, you are wearing grubby clothes, so it is okay for them to jump on you, as they approach, you open your arms and give the command "hugs". This is your on switch. When they jump up, and they will, you wrap your arms around them and hold them up on you. When they start to pull back-they are ready to get down, hold them on a few seconds longer. Then give the command "off", or "feet" and point to the floor. Give the off switch and release them to put all 4 feet on the floor. TRPP as soon as they have all 4 paws on the floor. You allowed them to give you the hug, but they did not get any treat or praise for it. You gave them the command for off and then they got the reward. This is the basis for any behavior you want to extinguish. Set them up, give it a name, the on switch, let them do it when given the command, give the off switch command and TRPP.

This is the first step for this, there is a second one. You need to replace the undesirable behavior with another one. You need to replace the behavior of jumping up when they approach you to sitting to get petted. You will again, set the training session up. Have one person with your companion on leash. As your companion approaches you, give the command to "sit". When your companion sits, TRPP. Repeat this exercise several times. When your companion begins to realize that sitting upon getting to you gets a treat and praise, as opposed to jumping on you, they will begin to make the choice for the proper behavior. This, like any issue you may face takes time and consistency to perfect/retrain/replace. Be patient and consistent and it will happen.

Many of these behaviors are what we term self-satisfying, so it is up to you to do the work to replace them with behaviors that will be less objectionable to all concerned. If it is a behavior that I know this particular dog really enjoys, jumping up, barking, for a few examples, I will make sure that I allow them to do it occasionally-as long as it is safe.

Behaviors such as chasing cats and cars are particularly hard to extinguish and will take due diligence on your part to overcome. It can be done; however, you may want to seek assistance from a professional if you find they are engrained behaviors in your adult rescue. This is one of the reasons you want to stop them before they get to this stage with your puppies. It will always be easier to change a behavior when it is starting than to have to change a behavior that has been around for a long time. Just as with a human, the longer something has been a "habit" the longer it will take to release that behavior and replace it with a desirable behavior.

LEAVE IT

Whether your companion is interested in food on the counter, a small child, a fuzzy kitten or anything else you have deemed unacceptable, "leave it" is a command they need to learn. It is best to start with a food treat in your hand, as this is something you can control. Put a food treat in your hand and make a fist. Hold the treat in front of your companion's nose with your fingers facing down. Give the command, "leave it" and wait for your companions to stop licking and nosing your hand. The instant they stop and look away, open your hand and give them the treat. Repeat this process many times in one session. It doesn't usually take long for the 4 leggers to figure out that the sooner they stop chewing on, poking at, licking, biting, etc., your hand, the sooner they get the cookie. Once they make this realization, it is time to move on to the next step. You want them to look at you-to not only look away from your hand-but to look at you for the cookie.

Now you will bring your hand with the cookie toward your eyes before you give it to your companion. This should bring their eyes to yours. As soon as your companion makes eye contact with you, give them the cookie. So the process is now to hold the cookie in your fist, give the command, "leave it", when they stop nudging, biting, licking, etc., your hand for the cookie, bring your fist to your face, toward your eyes and as soon as your companion makes eye contact, give them the cookie.

I like to take a little side step here and teach my companion:

WATCH

Sit your companion directly in front of you. You do want to be close to them so they do not have to work to make eye contact. If your companion is on the smaller side, sit them in a chair so you do not have to bend way over them. Looming over them can be intimidating to them and cause them to feel as if they are in a submissive position. If this is the case-they will be less apt to want to engage in eye contact with you. With your companion sitting in front of you, give the command "watch", and take the cookie from your eye, to your companion's nose and back to your eye and their nose. Repeat this action a couple of times to ensure that you have good eye contact. As soon as eye contact is established, give your companion the cookie. Here is another example of a time where you will become the cookie PEZ dispenser. Each time you give the command, you will want to quickly give the cookie and repeat the process. This will only last for a matter of a few minutes before you release and play with your companion. All through the process you will be treating and praising your companion, letting them know as you treat them that it is a good watch, each time they make eye contact. You want them to know that making eye contact is a good thing and will get them a cookie.

You can see that Mary is close to Jumelle's nose and that she is using both hands. This is so that she can have treats at the ready.

This may take some time with older dogs and especially males and dogs that have been abused. They can feel that they are challenging you or invading your space by making eye contact. You may have to work to convince them it is okay for them to make eye contact by asking for very short periods of contact and by using a soft focus with your eyes.

Once your companion has a good "watch", you can start to go on to the next step in the "leave it" process. Put your companion in a sit in front of you, just like you did for the watch training. Give the watch command and then drop a cookie a foot off to the right or left onto the floor as you give the "leave it" command. Repeat the "watch" command if your companion starts to go after the treat on the floor. Cover the treat with your foot to prevent them from getting the treat if they try to go after the treat on the floor. Repeat the "watch" command and use another treat to lure your companion back to your eyes. When your companion re-establishes eye contact, give them the treat. Give the "watch" command again, drop a treat and give the "leave it" command. As soon as they look at you, give them the treat from your hand-DO NOT allow them to get the treat off the floor. When you feel your companion is beginning to get the idea that looking at you gets the cookie, not diving toward the floor, you can leave out the "watch me" command and just give the "leave it" command and wait for them to look at you. When they look at you, reward them with several cookies the first time. This will let them know-without hesitation-they have made the right choice and that this is the choice they want to make again.

When they are consistently looking to you for the cookie when you say leave it as the cookies are falling to the floor, you are ready to progress to the next step. You can place cookies on the counter, on chairs, on the floor in front of them on a stay and give the "leave it" command. Have your companion on leash and walk past the location where you have left the treat. Give the "leave it" command as you come close to the treat. When your companion looks at you, as opposed to the treat, TRPP. Get creative and make a game out of this. Ultimately you will be able to use this to prevent your companion from taking food from a child, food off the counter, toys they should not play with, etc. Just be sure that they always get the treat from you. Never release them to get the "leave it" treat.

WITH ME

One of the goals for any owner and their companion is to be able to go for an enjoyable walk. An enjoyable walk for your companion is going to entail being able to sniff things and investigate nooks and crannies, follow leaves or butterflies, etc. Our idea of an enjoyable walk tends to be one where we are not jerked around by our companion on the other end of the leash. How do we come to a happy medium? Teaching your companion that they can go to the end of a 6 foot leash, but must come back when asked is the key. If you have ever observed a dog tied out on a length of chain? As unfortunate as this is to see, there is a lesson to be learned here. These dogs will go to the end of the chain and stop. They know exactly where the end of the chain is. This is the principle we want to instill in our companions when we go for a walk. We don't want to use the command "heel" as this means to walk at our side and stay there, so we will use something different, I use "with me". You can use whatever you want, just be sure it is not the same command as when you want your companion to heel alongside you.

I have found this is easiest taught using a flexi. When you drag the brake on the flexi it makes a clicking sound. I use this sound to start to condition the response to turn and come back to me. In the beginning I will only allow my companion to get a few feet away from me. I will drag the brake on the flexi and give a light tug on the flexi. At the same time that I give the light tug on the flexi I will give the command "come back". I am essentially asking my companion to check in with me. The verbal command "come back" lets them know they have gone far enough and I want them to check in. Eventually, when they are hearing the drag on the brake and turning to come back without me saying anything, I will start to allow them out farther. At this point I can generally take them out on a 6' leash and transfer the lesson using the light tug on the leash when they come to the end of the leash and adding the "come back" command when necessary. Any time you get into a situation where there are other dogs, a lot of people, traffic, etc., call your companion back into heel position for as long as you need to. When it is safe, give the "with me" command and proceed with your walk, allowing your companion to enjoy it as much as you are.

LIVING COMMANDS IN REVIEW:

1. Clothes on.
2. Bedtime.
3. On/Off switch.
4. Leave it.
5. Watch.
6. With me.

CHAPTER FIVE

OTHER ISSUES

FEAR/AGGRESSION

Aggression in puppies and rescues is in most cases fear based. Many times what starts out as a non-issue, becomes a major one due to the humans inability to look at this from the canine perspective. What could have been deescalated and forgotten became magnified by the reaction of the human to the canine behavior. At times it may be a physical issue, so the first thing to do is ALWAYS get a complete examination by your veterinarian, including blood work, and this should include a thyroid panel. If any health issue is excluded, it is most likely fear based and behavioral, and so needs to be addressed from a positive avenue. If this is a rescue with a severe fear/aggression issue, seek the help of a professional. By professional I am not just suggesting an obedience instructor. With this type of issue, you are going well beyond what basic obedience can do. Work to find a T-Touch practitioner, or some other type of professional that has been trained specifically to work with fear/aggression issues.

PROACTIVE AND POSITIVE

There are many ways fear can appear to be aggression. It can start as something so very simple. Here is one scenario: We have a young puppy in a training class. An over exuberant older, bigger puppy runs over and rolls the smaller younger puppy. It may not seem at the time that any damage is done, there may not have been any yelping, no physical damage was done, and there was certainly no bad intent on the part of the older larger puppy, however, psychologically, the younger pup got a bad taste in their mouth and as they proceed to get older, see every exuberant dog heading toward them as a threat, see themselves getting knocked over and rolled and answer the charge with hairs up and a growl-a message to slow down and back off. An inexperienced owner would see this as their wonderful puppy becoming aggressive toward other puppies/dogs, when in fact, this is only a fear issue. How would one best handle the situation? Very simply, step between your puppy and the approaching dog, talk to your puppy in a low and soothing voice, but a confident one, not one that is sympathetic to their "situation". Let them know it is your job to protect them, and you will do your job. Ask the person with the approaching puppy to please get their puppy under control and to hold their puppy so that yours may approach theirs-not the other way around. At the same time, smooth the hair on the back of your puppy's neck, put their tail in a neutral position, and approach the other canine at an arch, not a straight line. Allow your puppy to sniff the ground as you approach. Allow the two canines to meet nose to rear, as dogs do-to shake hands-and assure your puppy you have done your job to protect them, that this was a perfectly friendly pup, just a rather outgoing friendly sort. Praise your puppy for a job well done and walk away. This is what happened to Jahari when she was a pup in one of her first classes. At the time of this writing she is Sp-HIT Liberty's Jahari Heart CD,RE,CGC,TDI. She won the GDCA 2012 Novice Obedience Invitational Championship. Does she still get a little concerned if there are dogs getting too exuberant? Yes, but she looks to me to do my job. It is odd how one small incident in a puppy class could have such a lasting impression on her, but there it is and it is a striking example of how any situation, no matter what it looks like to us, can look very different to them.

This is yet another reminder of why positively reinforcing these types of issues is so important. Jerking on the leash, smacking your puppy on the nose, spraying your puppy in the face with water are all negative reinforcements. What you are in essence doing is letting them know that when another puppy comes around; something they are already unsure of to start with, something bad IS going to happen. The situation will get worse and eventually you will have a puppy that is now a dog with a real aggression issue-as opposed to a situation they may remember, but have not allowed it to become an issue.

COOKIE OBJECTS

Adding the watch command and positively reinforcing your puppy/rescue with cookies is another way to make the presence of another animal or human a positive as opposed to a negative experience.

Start with the "unfriendly object" at a comfortable distance to your puppy/rescue. This may truly be an object, vacuum, man, child, dog or cat, etc. Find out what the comfort zone is by noticing how far away the object needs to be such that your companion does not react to it's presence. Once this is established, have the object pass by, at that comfortable distance, while you give the command "watch". At the same time, mention the "cookie object" is passing by. I might be saying something like this; "Watch, good watch, is that your cookie person, that is a good cookie person, good watch, yes, there is my good watch, good cookie person, good watch." At which time, the person would pass out of sight, I would go quiet and the cookies would stop. The person would again come into view, staying just outside the comfort zone, and the process would be repeated. When you feel your companion has the idea that the appearance of the "object" produces cookies when they look at you, it is time to proceed to the next step. Have the "object" move just inside the comfort zone by one foot. The process is the same as before, but now the object is within the comfort zone. You may have to work harder to keep the "watch" and to keep good eye contact. If your companion is too uncomfortable with this step, back up and wait a little longer. As your companion becomes comfortable with each progression, have the object move closer. Take this slowly. Don't ask for too much too soon. Don't make the mistake of wanting to do it ONE MORE TIME. Quit while you are ahead. There is always tomorrow. If you push too much, you will have taken 3 giant steps backwards and it isn't worth it. Slow and steady sets the pace and will accomplish the task.

TREAT RETREAT

One other method that works when working with fear/aggression issues with people is treat/retreat. I generally use this method in conjunction with T-Touch, but it can be used alone. I feel it is more effective if used with T-Touch, however.

Start with your companion on leash, you will be holding the leash. The person will be how ever many feet away that they need to be to be outside the comfort zone. For this example, let's say it is 20'. The person will throw your companions favorite treat, a large enough piece so that they can see it between the two of you, at the ½ way point, 10 feet. You will allow your companion to go to get the treat. As your companion goes toward the treat, the person will back up the same distance. Treat/retreat. When your companion is comfortable with this process, you can move to step two.

The next step in this process is to throw the treat 1/2 the distance between the two of you, but instead of backing up the full distance, 10 feet, the person would only back up 8 feet. You will allow your companion to go toward the treat and get it, but the person would be backing up 8 feet instead of 10 feet. You will maintain this distance until your companion is comfortable with this distance.

You continue to progress and the gap will continue to close, but it is the canine that is closing the gap, not the human. Eventually your companion should feel comfortable coming up to the person and taking the treat from their hand. Be sure the person is standing sideways, and not looking at them, not trying to make eye contact at the time. As before, take it slow. This can happen in one session, or it could take weeks. It depends on how deep set the fear issue is. It is also dependant upon how much trust has been built between you and your companion.

Working on fear/aggression issues is something that should be left to work on until your relationship has had a little time to develop. Take the time to get to know one another first. Establish trust and spend some time bonding with each other.

Fear/Aggression Issues

1. Proactive and positive.
2. Cookie objects.
3. Treat/retreat.

At any time you feel you need assistance, do seek out the help of a professional. T-Touch is wonderful for working with fear/aggression issues and there are many qualified practitioners that can be found all over the United States as well as many other countries. Do not limit yourself to the T-Touch web site-they only list practitioners that pay to be listed there. Many are available by word of mouth. So look around and ask horse people as well as your canine friends. It will be well worth the effort if you have this issue and need assistance in dealing with it.

BITE INHIBITION

I ran into a friend wearing band aides all over her hands and arms. She explained she had a new puppy and it had teeth like little razors-don't they all? We talked about bite inhibition, and that this little package seemed to have none. It is amazing to me the number of puppies and rescues that do not have proper bite inhibition. This is one of the basics that must be instilled to save a dogs life. I have spoken of Calista before; she was one Dane that was returned to me due to lack of proper care and training on the part of her previous owners. She was a mess, but at least due to proper bite inhibition training on my part, although she had been abused through ignorance with a prong collar, she would put her mouth on the abuser, but she never put any pressure on, never caused a bruise, she was just warning or asking the person to please stop hurting her. Had she not had proper bite inhibition, she could have caused a lot of damage.

I do want to be clear here, I am talking about a bite inhibition problem, not a dog with an aggressive bite problem. I am not encouraging anyone to work with a dog that is aggressive-whether it is fear based aggression or not doesn't matter-with an established bite problem or a history of biting. I would never advocate the placement of a rescue with a history of serious biting. This is best left to the professionals to deal with. There is a world of difference between a puppy or rescue that just doesn't realize how hard they are biting and one that is lashing out from fear/aggression and is intent on doing damage. To give you an example of what I am talking about: I brought in a Rottweiler rescue at one time. This poor fellow had been so badly abused that he was missing a chunk of his skull. He was covered in feces when I found him, we had to cut the choke chain out of his neck and he was quite thin and severely food aggressive. At one point, near the food bowl, he did put his mouth on my hand-I was a good foot away from his bowl- but it was a bite release, he had good bite inhibition, I am glad to say. His intent, although he was food aggressive, and he did not want anyone to take his food away, was to protect his food at all costs, not to do harm. He had good bite inhibition and although he made full contact, he did not even leave a bruise. I have to admit, the look on his face after the fact was such that I do believe he regretted what he had done and he and I became the best of friends. Barnaby ended up staying with me until the day he died at the ripe old age of approximately 14. (Assuming he was about a year old when I found him.)

When there is a bite inhibition issue, no matter the age, the process to solve the problem is the same. Unfortunately, you have to allow the biting to some degree in the beginning. You need to be sure you are somewhat protected, I make sure I am wearing sleeves and gloves and allow myself to get chewed on. I play with the dog with the biting issue, just as they would play with another dog.

When they start to bite hard, and you want to push them to bite hard, yell "OUCH", very loudly. Immediately stop the play, walk out of the room, or play area for 5-10 minutes. Do not say anything, do not scold them, do not give them any attention positive or negative. What you want them to realize is that they have put their mouth on you-too hard, and this stops the play. You will leave, you are not having fun and you will stop the play time and go away. YOU GO AWAY. This is their "punishment" as it were, that you, the toy, is taken away. You do not want to isolate them, to put them in a time out, YOU want to be the one to leave. As this "game" progresses, you will begin to yell "OUCH" and leave when they apply less pressure. Eventually you will yell "OUCH" nearly as soon as they put their mouth on you. They will begin to think that humans are very delicate creatures indeed! This process does take time, but it is well worth the effort.

TUG

As with every behavior, there is a step two. When you want to extinguish one behavior, you must replace it with another. Putting things in their mouths is just part of what dogs do. Allowing them to do this and making it a game, but insuring that you control the game, you instigate the game, you control the toy and you end the game are all part and parcel what make it work.

Pick a tug toy that is size appropriate for your companion. Make sure that it is long enough and big enough around for you to get a hold of and hang onto without getting your fingers pinched. You also want to be sure your companion can grab at it without risk of getting your fingers or hand or arm by accident. This is a toy that will only come out when you choose to instigate the game of tug.

This toy will not be out all the time for your companion to play with. You will bring out the toy and give the command "tug". Play tug with your companion and allow them at this time to put their mouth on this toy and pull just as hard as they want to. It is also okay to allow them to "win" once in awhile. In other words, let them pull the toy out of your hands. Make a big deal out of the fact that they won. "You got it, you got it. Good for you. Okay, let's play again. Come tug." Let them win 1 out of 5 times that you tug. The other 4 times, tell them to "give" or "out" and make them release the toy to you. Offer them a treat and praise them when they release the tug toy to you. When you are finished playing, you end the game, let them know you are done and put the toy away.

TUG WITH OTHER OBJECTS

When they have learned good bite inhibition and they have learned to play tug with the tug toy-and by learned, I mean that they follow the rules by giving you the tug when asked to do so-you can transfer the tug game to other things. If they are getting bored while at the veterinarians office, you can fold up your leash and play tug with that. You can use a towel, any toy, your leash, etc., as long as they understand the rules and will "give" when asked.

BITE INHIBITION ISSUES

1. OUCH-you leave the play area.
2. Tug game with one specific toy.
3. Tug with other objects.

STAIRS

Does this sound like an odd topic? This is not usually an issue for the smaller breeds, if they have a problem with stairs, they can be carried, however, if this is an issue with the medium to larger breeds, this can be an issue. There are a number of breeds that depending on how they were raised, where they were raised, or for reasons due to injury etc., either were not allowed to do stairs, could not do stairs or just never had the opportunity to do stairs. For some dogs stairs can appear to be a rather daunting scary undertaking. We have to remember to look at them from the dogs perspective.

This is again, where the 4 P's of puppy training will come into play. There can be no time table, no hidden agenda. Literally you must plan to take things one step at a time. Most dogs can do 4 or 5 stairs without an issue. When they take those few stairs and they become a long tall staircase it becomes an entirely different issue. Whether this is due to the height, length or other such appearance of said staircase, I do not know, what I do know is that this is a situation that is easily over come, but it takes patience and calm on the part of the human. Put your emotions aside and settle in to whatever time table your canine companion has in store. Rome was not built in a day and neither will your companion master stairs.

Age also plays an important role in how quickly they become comfortable with stairs. Older dogs may catch on faster than puppies simply because they are more coordinated. As much as this seems odd, also think in terms of the size of the dog compared to the size of the stairs? Also remember that an older dog has had many more experiences to draw upon and a puppy has had so few. Trying to coordinate-again thinking large puppy-all 4 limbs to get up a very long set of stairs, and then back down, can be a rather daunting experience. Each dog is different and each experience will be different. Some may catch on in one 20 minute session; others may take several over a period of days.

TOUCH

Depending on the severity of the issue, you may need to teach all of these steps, or maybe just the first one. The first step I teach is touch. This is very simple, but gets the idea across to put a foot on something. Use a board painted a different color than the regular surface. If you don't have a board, you can even use a folded up bath mat. Give the command "touch", point to the board and when your companion puts a foot on the board reward with a cookie and praise them while they are on the board. Give your release command. The cookie and praise will come while they are on the board, not after the release command. Repeat this process several times. When you get to the point in the process that you can give the "touch" command and your companion will put both front feet on the board and stand there until you give the release command-don't ask for too much, just 5 seconds or so, you are ready to move on to the next step. Again, you may or may not need this step, but if you do, it is not hard to teach.

Most will start up the stairs with just the "touch" command. This will get their front feet on the stairs. Many will get their front feet as far up the stairs as they can go and still have their hind feet on the floor. With large Great Dane puppies/rescues this can have them nearly 1/3 of the way up the staircase! This is the point where patience, encouragement, praise and T-Touch come in VERY handy.

STEP

For step two you will need a long board, 10 X 12. Paint one end the same color as the board you used for "touch". Now you are going to use the command "step". Give the "touch" command and your companion will know to touch the colored zone on the end of the board. From this point you will tell them to "step". Encourage them with a cookie in front of their nose to take just one step across the board. At this point it doesn't matter if they keep all 4 feet on it, just take 1 step across it, etc. The point is that they take 1 step. Give them the cookie, release them and repeat the process. Continue this process until they will step all the way across the board.

THE STAIRS-UP

Once they understand "touch" and "step" you are ready to take this to the stairs. You will want to bring an extra good cookie for this part of the process. Bring something that is extra tasty and hard to resist. Start going up as this is easier than going down. If you have a staircase such that you can go up and not have to go down that is the best way to start. Give the command "touch" and have your companion put both front feet on the bottom step. They should be fairly comfortable with this. Reward them for this. Give the command "step". They may hesitate at this point. It is okay. Encourage them with the cookie. Any movement forward should be rewarded. Remember to keep any negative emotions at 0. In other words, don't get frustrated, don't get angry, don't give up. Remember to accept what you get as great and positive.

Understand that it may come in one session, it may take 10, it will take what it takes. I had an adult Dane, Bon Jovi, that I decided to do agility with after he finished his championship. He loved everything but the dog walk. I worked with him for over a year and he just couldn't get it. He had no problem jumping off of it if he was the least bit concerned that he might fall off, and would go faster if he got concerned-at which point he would get wide in the rear-not what you want on that narrow board. I finally decided we would just do jumpers and not do standard, the part of agility with the contact obstacles. The dog walk was in the ring where we trained and he would generally put his feet on it as we passed by, which I never discouraged, just told him it was a good touch and went on. One day he just walked on up, over and down the other side! We had a big party on the other side. He has been doing the dog walk ever since. The point is, I didn't make an issue out of it, I allowed him space to do it if and when he wanted and he finally decided it was okay.

Back to the stairs. It is better if you can find a shorter staircase to start with and build on it, but that isn't usually the way it is. Getting half way up isn't usually an option either. So once you start, getting to the top is generally the goal. Make sure you have time to devote to the project. You don't want to push and cause a worse problem. Patience is the key. Start with one step, ask for the next step, then one more. Be prepared to sit on each step for some time to allow them to adjust. STAY BESIDE THEM. DO NOT GET IN FRONT OF THEM. If you feel the need to help them move a foot, do so, but gently pick up the foot and place it on the step. Don't grab it and jerk it up onto the step. Talk to them and let them know what you are doing. Use a low soothing voice. It might sound something like this, "Okay, you seem a bit stuck, I am going to help, just a little. I am going to lift your left back leg and set it on the step for you. There, that wasn't so tough was it?"

They also need to understand that going backwards isn't an option, up is the only way to go. I want to stress here that you don't want to get into a big fight on the stairs and get the dog hurt, which is why you take this slow and easy and do not push. BUT-especially when you get started at the bottom, when it is easy for them to back out-if they start to back up, one step, one foot back and forth is okay, this you can ignore. If they want to move away from the stairs, this is not acceptable. Keep them at the stairs. If they pull on the leash, keep the tension there, let them know you need them to stay with you at the stairs. Some may be adamant that they want away from the stairs, especially puppies or rescues that have learned that pitching a fit will get them what they want, be gentle, but firm in your resolve-no emotion! Hold them steady, use a soothing voice and when they are quiet, continue, just as if it had never happened. Puppies can be pretty good at thrashing about on the end of the leash when they don't want to do something. This can look very frightening to a novice owner. Don't give in to the appearance of your puppy throwing a temper tantrum. Again, be gentle, but firm, hold your ground, proceed as soon as they are finished, as if it had never happened. Just remember not to allow them to back away. Once they get started up the stairs, they will generally stay where they are, maybe stepping back with their front feet a step, but if you stay with them, keep the leash loose, (I generally don't even have a hold of it, it is dropped and on the steps.), they will eventually make it to the top.

This is also a situation where I feel something like using T-Touch can be extremely beneficial. I know I have mentioned this several times, but when you are working with rescues, or any issues that need a calming hand, T-Touch is worth it's weight in gold for helping both you and your companion. T-Touch has the benefit of helping both the one receiving the Touch as well as the one giving the Touch. Books and videos can be purchased online and I would highly recommend learning at least the basics for your personal use. If you have the added benefit of a T-Touch practitioner close at hand, work with them. It is worth the time and financial expenditure. They will teach you some techniques hands on-much better than trying to learn from a video if you have that access.

As well as having a cookie in my hand and giving them the treat when them go forward, I will also have a large cookie on the step ahead of them where they have to reach for it-to take a step up-to get to it. This encourages them to always be looking up and working toward the next step.

Once you get to the top of the stairs, I will have a special play time with my companion. It has to be worth getting there. Play tug, play chase outside, play a retrieval game, something that is special to this individual. Have something at the top of the stairs that is a great and wonderful surprise for them to find.

Depending on how the session went, you may want to repeat the session or call it a day. If it took 5 minutes to get to the top, if the tail was wagging the whole time, it just took concentration on their part and encouragement on yours, you may want to repeat the process 2 or 3 more times to get them going smoothly up to the top and after 20 minutes they may have it down. If it took 20 minutes to get them up the first time, if you are exhausted, if you had to lift each foot, you may want to call it a day and try again tomorrow.

I had a deaf puppy, Wizard, I had placed him with a very sweet young man that took him home and returned him 2 days later due to his inability to get him to do the stairs at his home. He was very upset, feeling overwhelmed. He had "worked" for a day with little success, potty accidents and emotional upheaval on his part. I took Wizard back and told him I would work on the "issue" and we would talk. I spent 20 minutes with Wizard, had him going up the stairs with ease. It wasn't Wizard's issue. The owner was getting emotional, the puppy was getting concerned and it was a mess. You must keep your emotions out of the picture. Wizard is was a very smart puppy, a quick learner. He was confused by the emotions of his new owner, so many new things in his new environment. He could do stairs, 5 or 6, had never had to do an entire staircase, Wizard just needed the proper encouragement, patience and praise.

Unlike other issues, one session a day on the stairs is plenty. It can be rather hard on the joints of puppies and you don't want them to get sore and associate that with the stairs. One rule to follow here is not to overdo. If you can work on going up in one session and going down in another that is preferable. Most will master the stairs in one session. For those that need more than one session, remember patience and praise.

THE STAIRS-DOWN

Going down stairs can be even more daunting than going up. This is also harder on the joints of growing large breed puppies. The process is the same as going up, except that it <u>may</u> take longer, you do want to go slower to ensure they do not fall and injure themselves. I say may because each puppy/rescue is different. Be sure that you do not pull them down the stairs. Be patient, allow them to go down at their pace. Place the cookie on the step below them and wait for them to take a step down onto that step to get the cookie. Give the "touch" command and point to the step. They may stay on that first step for quite some time before deciding to proceed. I like to place several cookies on the next step and the next one so that they can see them. I'll even have them watch me drop several in a large pile a couple of steps below where they are standing. For going down stairs, as opposed to going up the stairs, you will be in front of your companion; there is just no other way to do it. I do not allow them to back away from the top of the stairs. They may step back and forth off of the top step several times, this is normal. I will reward them each and every time they come back onto the first step. Patience is really the key here. I find that once they get onto the second step or so most of them just go right on past me and go all the way to the bottom of the stairs without ceremony.

STAIRS

1. Touch.
2. Step.
3. Stairs. Up then Down.

BATHING

I find it amusing that dogs will roll in dead things, jump into filthy ponds, ice cold with muddy bottoms, but bring on clean warm water and soap and they run like the devil is after them. Most dogs will have to accept bathing, so making it a pleasant experience it conducive to all involved.

INTRODUCING WATER

The best way to introduce most dogs to bathing is outside with a hose. I like to start with another dog that likes water and likes to play with the hose. I make a game of it-starting on a hot day in the summer is a given. Get the dogs to bite at and play with the water coming out of the hose and to drink from the hose. While this game is going on take the opportunity to gently spray the dogs bodies now and then with the hose. Any dog that is used to playing the game will be right in the middle of things. Dogs new to the game will be on the outside watching. They may or may not take part at first, but dogs are dogs and you will find that they don't like to be excluded. Eventually they will want to be a part of the game and they will come close enough to take part. What you don't want to do is surprise spray them. Don't make any sneak attacks with the hose. If the come through the spray, great. If not, don't worry about it. Eventually they will, whether by choice or accident as they play with the other dog(s).

If you don't have another dog to teach them, you can start by running the hose outside and watering flowers or grass, using a sprinkler and running through it yourself, etc. Get creative. There are a lot of ways to start to introduce dogs to water that do not at first involve a bath.

Once your companion is used to water, then you can use it with a purpose. It is preferable to start outside if that is an option. I know that many people only have a tub to bathe their dogs in, getting dogs in and out of a tub can be the first obstacle, this is why getting them to like the bath is first-getting them in and out of the tub is second.

THE BATH OUTSIDE

Be sure to have them on leash. There is nothing worse than getting the process started and having your companion run off with soap all over them. Check the temperature of the water. Be sure it is warm, not cold or too hot. Start by running the water over their legs. The first session this may be all that you do.

You want the bath to be a positive experience, so doing it in small steps is important. Once they are comfortable with having their legs hosed off, move to the chest area. Be sure you are not using the spray, just the hose running on them at this point. Allow them to get a drink out of the hose if they want to.

Once they are comfortable with the legs and the chest, progress to the sides, then the back and finally the rear. When you can run the hose over the whole body, you can start to allow it to spray lightly on the legs and chest. When they are comfortable with this part of the process, then go over the whole body with the spray. From here you can add soap and a "body massage". Some dogs seem to think it is a bit strange when all the white stuff starts coming off of them-the soap bubbles. They get used to this fairly quickly, but just be prepared if you have one of those that is worried about the white stuff on the ground and is trying to step out of it.

SHAKE OFF

Finally I teach my 4 leggers to "shake off". I hold the towel between the two of us and give the command "shake off". Some times you have to be patient, but hold the towel and wait. Stand with the towel between you and the dog until they shake off all the water from the bath. Praise them when they do-and they will, and then towel them off. This is so that they will shake off the majority of the water and I can towel them dry. Then they will go into the house so they won't get dirty. When they are getting bathed in the house, I can tell them to shake off before getting out of the tub, the majority of the water and mess will stay in the tub, not all over me or the floor, and then they can step out of the tub, I can tell them to shake off again and I can proceed to finish to towel them dry.

THE TUB

Once your companion is enjoying the bath, you are ready to move to the bath tub. I put one of the hand sprayers on the tub. It has the massager and well as a sprayer. I had one dog that enjoyed his baths so much that anytime I could not find him, all I had to do was go look in the bathroom and there he was, in the tub! Stetson was a great dog for teaching others to love a bath as well. He would crowd in front of the hose any time it was on.

This is another time where "touch" and "step" can come in handy. Point to the edge of the tub and give the "touch" command. Then give the "step" command and encourage them to get into the tub. Many dogs that have not been bathed in the tub will take great offence at having to get into a tub. Once you get the front feet in the tub, be patient, praise them for getting the front end in the tub. Remind them that they are going to get a bath. If you start with the front end near the rear of the tub, give the touch command and step command, now have the front feet in the tub, and now ask again for them to step, moving them toward the front of the tub, they will start to move in that direction. Many will continue to move the front end, and not the rear. The first time they get in the tub, you may need to set the back feet in the tub, so it will help to have a second person at the head to keep the front feet in while you put the back feet in. If you are working alone, and I usually am, be sure you have a leash on them. If the front end gets out of the tub while you are putting the back end in, no big deal, just start again and know that now they have had all 4 feet in the tub and it did not harm them, so it should be easier to get there again. Just as with the stairs, patience and praise.

THE BATH INSIDE

Once you get them in the tub, the process is the same with the water as it was outside. Start by merely running it over their legs. Don't plan on giving them a bath if they seem at all concerned. Only progress as long as they seem to understand that this is the same bath process that they already love. Allow them to drink the water from the sprayer, just as they did outside. They need to understand that this is just water. You also want to ensure that the surface, both inside the tub and outside is safe and non-skid so they will not slip or feel unsafe. The last thing you want is for them to slip and hurt themselves getting in or out of the tub. There are several places that carry non-slip applique's which can be applied to the bottom of the tub. I find these much better than the rubber mats which are supposed to stick to the bottom of the tub. Most dogs are large enough that if they start moving around will get them wadded up and they won't do any good. Most dogs will find bathing a pleasant experience at best and tolerable at worst. You want to ensure they don't slip and feel unsafe, that the water temperature is to their liking, that they do not get scalded or that it is cold and unpleasant. You want to be sure not to get shampoo in their eyes, water in their ears or up their noses etc. In general you want to make the entire bathing experience as pleasant as possible.

BATHING

1. Introducing water.
2. The bath outside.
3. Shake off.
4. The tub.
5. The bath inside.

NAILS

As a T-Touch Practitioner this is probably one of the most common issues I have had people tell me they have had with their dogs. As a breeder, I see this as a complete non-issue. I start doing my puppies nails when they are a few days old and continue to do them weekly from then on. Even with this practice I find that when I send my puppies home my puppy owner can slack off and end up with puppies/adults with horrid looking nails, with issues having their nails done. Why you ask-simple; because the owners allowed these puppies to tell them no. As simple as this sounds, once the puppy was in a new environment, with new humans, they decided to test the water. When the new owners went to do their nails they struggled a little, the owners, loving their new puppy, not wanting their new puppy not to love them, relented. This was mistake number one. Now said puppy thinks, hmm, this got me what I wanted, next time I will struggle harder-and so it goes until there is now an issue with getting the nails done. If only the new puppy owner had held on a little tighter, proceeded with the dremmeling of the nails, said puppy would have given a sigh, gotten their nails done and not struggled at all on the next session.

The question now is how to undo what has been done. Of course there are those that are bad about having their nails done just because they have not had them done, or because they have had them done improperly or for what ever reason, but the way to fix the issue is the same. NOW I will preface all of this by saying, if you have access to a T-Touch practitioner, GO. It is money well spent. One or two sessions will give you the training you need and save you a lot of time and energy. Sorry to keep harping on this, but if it works?

INTRODUCING THE DREMMEL

For those without access, here is the next best thing. Be sure you have your companion in a location where they cannot get away. You either want them on a chair, in a corner, in your lap, some place or somehow such that you have a hold of them and you have them under control. Start with a battery operated dremmel. They are quieter. Present the dremmel and allow your companion to sniff it. Give a treat each time they sniff or touch it.

Now you need for them to allow the dremmel to touch them, specifically their nails. Start with just the foot. Touch the dremmel to their foot and give them a treat. Touch/treat/touch/treat/touch treat. Do this with all four feet. When they are willingly accepting the dremmel touching each foot, progress to touching the nails. You want to hold the foot in such a way that they nail will be extended. To do this you will hold the paw with your fingers under the paw and your pointer finger under the pad of the toe you are working on. Your thumb will gently press on the joint of the toe you are working on. Try this. You will see how this causes the nail on that toe to come out so that you can more easily get to it. If your companion has a really hard time even having their feet handled, stop here and work with their feet for a short time. Just hold them, caress them and give them a cookie. Work for them to allow you to handle them for longer periods of time before you progress.

DREMMEL NOISE

Once your companion is accepting the dremmel touching each nail, it is time to get them to accept the noise of the dremmel. Move the dremmel a good distance from them. If you have two people this works best as you can move it a good comfortable distance. If you are working by yourself, hold it as far away as you can. Turn the dremmel on and give them a treat while it is on. Turn it off. Turn it on and give them a treat, turn it off. It is important that they get the treat while the dremmel is on, not after it is turned off. This can be a little tricky when you are working alone, especially if your companion is sensitive to the sound, but do the best you can. As you see that your companion is comfortable with this distance gradually move the dremmel closer until you can turn it on and off right next to them.

DREMMEL TOUCH

Now you are ready to turn it on and touch them with it. With your hand between your companion and the dremmel, touch their foot with the dremmel and give them a treat. Dremmel on/touch/treat/repeat. Do this for each foot.

When they are comfortable with this step, you are ready to move on to touching their nails. Keep in mind that you will not be dremmeling their nails yet, just touching them with the dremmel. Dremmel on/touch/treat/repeat. Do this for each nail.

Take your time, progress in each session as you see that your companion is comfortable. End each session on a good note. Start each new session one step back from where you ended the previous one. If they struggle, simply follow their paw with your hand, don't clamp down on them, hold on, but don't grab on. I know this sounds strange, you want to follow their movement, keeping your hand on their paw, don't let go, but don't increase the pressure as this causes them to want to struggle more. When they discover they aren't getting anywhere they will give in.

Once they have accepted the touch of the dremmel while it is on and are staying quiet throughout the process, you will be able to proceed to actually getting on with the job of doing their nails. Depending on how long their nails are, it may take some time to get them back to a normal length, but you don't want to hit the quick as this is painful, so be conservative and take your time.

Whether it takes 3 sessions or 10, eventually, with persistence, you will have a companion that will sit or stand quietly while they have their nails dremmeled.

NAILS

1. Introducing the dremmel.
2. Dremmel noise.
3. Dremmel touch.

FOOD AGGRESSION/OBJECT GUARDING

Although these seem like separate issues, they are similar in that the dog guards the "item" as theirs when in fact, it is yours. What I mean is, they will protect said item from everyone else, including you, not allowing anyone or anything near it-guarding it from being "stolen". They are protecting their property, what they see as something they need to keep for theirs and only theirs.

Whether it is a food issue because they are afraid they may or may not have a next meal coming, as in Barnaby's situation, or just that they were raised with numerous littermates and never felt quite full and now have their own bowl and want to ensure that they get it all to themselves-does not matter. If it is a toy or bone issue and they feel they want to have it all to themselves and no one else is allowed to be near them or to have it, it is the same principle. The principle being, they want it and don't want anyone else to get it and feel they have the right to do so. Here in is their mistake.

EVERYTHING IS MINE

I live in a multi-Dane household. There is one big rule that we all must live by: Everything is MINE. The food is mine, the toys are mine, the bones are mine, the sitting and sleeping places are mine-you get the idea. This is rule number one. First and foremost all dogs in the house must understand that everything is mine, therefore, there is no reason for any of them to fuss over anything, it isn't theirs to start with. Once this is understood, all is good.

How does one go about bringing this understanding? Simple really. Before presenting the food, toys, etc., your companion must work for them. Ask them to sit before setting down the food bowl.

Release them to go and eat. All my puppies, even when there was a litter of 14 had to sit before I would put the bowls down. They knew this behavior before they went to their new homes. You will be teaching your new companion sit right from the start, so getting them to do something as simple as sit before putting the food bowl down is not hard to do. Give the release command, and allow them quiet time to eat. If your companion doesn't like other dogs around them when they eat and they get snarky, this is something you can work on.

FOOD AGGRESSION

Barnaby was severely food aggressive. In the beginning I would have to put a long line on him, run him to the back of the crate, hold his head to the rear of the crate while I put his food bowl in, release him after I shut the crate door to ensure I didn't get bitten. After we had been together for a few weeks I could set his bowl in before he went in and he would go past it and turn around in the crate and I could close the crate door without him growling and snapping. Eventually, over time, he realized I was going to feed him, I was not going to take it away, and he no longer growled at feeding time or around his bowl. I felt I could have reached in and picked it up if I wanted to BUT I never did. Why would I? In Barnaby's situation, knowing what he had come from, or suspecting at any rate, I had worked very hard to gain his trust, there was no reason to push it. It was enough to know that he was comfortable eating and having my hand setting his bowl down in front of him without issue.

How did we get to this point? One step at a time. Along with the basic obedience training he was getting, he was getting fed multiple times a day-food was always coming. I started with his head at the back of the crate with the bowl going in at the front and then releasing him. When he got used to me and could see his bowl wasn't going anywhere, the long line was removed and he could go into the crate with the bowl already in place. From there he progressed to sitting in front of the crate with the bowl in place and being released to go into the crate. The final step was to have the bowl in my hand, have him sit in front of the crate, release him to go into the crate and to set the bowl in the crate after he was in the crate. (He was always crated to eat so that he felt safe and knew the other dogs would not get his food.)

For puppies and rescues that do not have a food aggression issue and when you want to prevent this issue, start at a time that is not feeding time. Take the food bowl and put a few pieces of the regular kibble in it. Sit your companion. Set the food bowl down and release them to the bowl. Reach down and pick up the bowl. Show them that you have an extra good treat in your hand. This needs to be something big and really good. Chicken, steak, cheese, something they will really like and a big hunk of it. Put this treat in the bowl and make a big deal of doing it. Set the bowl back down. The idea that you are trying to convey is that if someone puts their hand near your bowl, and even if your bowl disappears, it will reappear with something even better. When your companion is comfortable with you doing this, have friends and strangers do the same thing.

OBJECT GUARDING

Whether it is a toy or a bone, or it could even be you-I have seen this when a rescue is particularly protective of the human that has saved them-it is never pleasant to see your loving companion turn into a snarling mess of gnashing teeth over a fluffy stuffed toy.

If you see that you have this issue, first be sure that your companion has good bite inhibition. If not, work on this issue first. Either way, be sure that your hands and arms are properly protected, just in case. Wear heavy leather gloves and make sure you have long sleeves covering your arms. You will also want to attach a string to the object you will be working with as another safety measure. This will ensure you do not have to place your hands directly in harms way if your companion is an extreme guarder.

RENFORCING LEAVE IT

You should have already been working on leave it. Spend a session or two reinforcing "leave it". You want to be sure that your companion had a good grasp of what this command means and that when you give this command, they will respond. Be sure to reward generously when they respond. You want to reward with something extra special, not the usual treat. You are going to be taking away something they want to keep later, so you need to let them know now that the reward they may be getting will be worth it.

TWO TOY GAME

You need to go and purchase several toys that are identical. You will have several sets of toys to work with. Attach strings to every toy. This is so that if your companion does not release the toy when asked, you have a little extra leverage without the potential of getting bitten. Start with two identical toys and special cookies in your pocket. Toss one toy for your companion to play with. When they are interested in toy #1, start trying to get them interested in toy #2. Give them the, "Look what I have.", conversation. Encourage them to come and get the toy you have. When it appears they are about to do so, give the "leave it" command and offer them toy #2. If they do not want to relinquish toy #1 offer toy #2 again and use the string if you need to on toy #1 to bring it back to you. You can also offer the really special cookie-yes a bribe if necessary- to get them to relinquish toy #1 and take toy #2. When they give up toy #1 and go after toy #2 give them a ton of praise and let them know they have done a good thing. For a dog that object guards, this is not easy. Now repeat this process going from toy #2 to toy #1.

You will go back and forth between the two toys several times. Always being sure to give a ton of praise for relinquishing the toy. When you are ready to quit the game, you will need for your companion to give up both toys. Remember you own everything in the end. For the final "leave it", you will offer the special cookie for the toy and use your end of training session command. You will then put both toys away. Game over.

The next time you play the game use two different toys. This way they will learn to transfer it to not only those two toys, but other toys as well. This is why you will want about 4 sets of these identical toys.

TAKE IT/GIVE EXCHANGE

You should now be able to progress to the phase where you can offer them a toy or bone, saying "take it" and allowing them to go off with it for a short time. Allow them 10 or 15 minutes with their toy or bone alone to enjoy it and then call them away from it and have your special treat ready. If they bring it with them, tell them to "give" and exchange the treat for the object. Return the object to them and allow them to go back and enjoy it for another 10 to 15 minutes. If they have done what is ideal and left the object behind, give them the treat and praise them for coming to you and release them to go back to their object. The best time to work on this type of training is in the evening while you are watching your favorite show. During every commercial break call your companion away from their object. If they seem hesitant to come away from the object, put a leash on them and go to them and call them to come and bring them to your location. In other words, if it is just too darned hard for them to tear themselves away, help them.

GIVE

Now that you know that you can exchange one toy for another-the two toy game, you can call them away from their object, it is time for you to get them to understand that you are also allowed to take the object away, should you choose to do so. They need to understand that you are the giver and also the taker of all things. What follows is that if they react properly, you are then the giver backer. Sorry for the improper English, but you get my point.

Start with something that will be rather benign. You do not want to use their favorite object. Use an old sock, a bandana tied in a knot, old scarf, etc., NOT their favorite stuffy or bone. With your companion sitting in front of you give the command "take it" and offer them the object. Play tug with them with the object or a few minutes. Give the command "give". If they do not immediately release the object stand very still, offer them a treat, not the great high value treats you have been previously using, just the regular treats and if need be slide you finger to the back of their mouth, behind their teeth and pry a little to get them to loosen their grip and open their mouth so you can get the object. Praise them when they give you the object. Keep working on this until you get a good release when you say "give".

The hardest part is yet to come. Transferring this to any time your companion has an object and you need to be able to take and give it back. You will need to find them with their object and go to them and give the command "give". They should immediately release the object to you. If they do, great! Give them a treat, praise them and immediately give it back. Be sure to praise them lavishly and leave them with their object. If they do not, give the "leave it" command, take the object for 5 to 10 minutes before returning it to them. They will begin to see that the sooner they relinquish it, the sooner they get it back. If at any time they growl or snap at you, you will take the object and put it away and they will not get it back for several hours.

Many people wonder why this is so important. If you have an only dog, if you never have company over, if small children are never near your dog then this is most likely not an issue and you don't need to worry about it. If on the other hand you do have another dog, there are likely to be children around, you do have friends and relatives over and want your dog in the vicinity during visits, I do strongly suggest working to resolve this issue so that you do not have a bite incident.

FOOD AGGRESSION/OBJECT GUARDING

1. Food aggression.
2. Safety first.
3. Feeding in a crate.
4. Reinforcing leave it.
5. Two toy game.
6. Take it/Give exchange.
7. Give.

OTHER ISSUES IN REVIEW

1. Fear/aggression.
2. Bite inhibition.
3. Bathing.
4. Nails.
5. Food aggression/Object guarding.

About The Author

My training career started with horses, but it was an easy transition to dogs. I trained my dogs in the beginning because they were rather large, Great Danes, and no one wanted a big dog that was not well behaved. I ran a training and boarding stable and always had my Danes by my side. I enjoyed training, no matter the species, so I continued to pursue it. I rode and trained horses from an early age and was competitive in many disciplines. My heart was devoted to Dressage and Eventing. The wide range of experiences gave me a fantastic base to draw upon when I started training dogs. I had worked with a variety of personalities and learned to adapt and change according to the needs of the animal I was working with.

My training was fairly informal, although there had been some opportunity to attend training classes, a few private lessons, a few seminars, reading books and watching others at shows, much of my learning has come from my Danes themselves. (I am a huge fan of Ian Dunbar and follow his philosophies.) I competed with my horses, but had no desire to compete with my Danes, despite all the training. Eventually, however, I was drawn in and as they say, once bitten...............

After a tragic fire and great loss took my stables and many of my beloved horses, my life took a slightly different turn. I had been to college at one time with a focus on my pre-vet, so added alternative therapy training after the fire, as much perhaps for my healing as for the benefit of healing the 4-leggers around me. My attention was as much on emotional and spiritual healing as it was on physical healing.

I also began to turn my attention to my Danes and as I had been competing with them in obedience and conformation, expanded now into agility, tracking, therapy and rally.

I was living with my "clan" or pack if you will and as such was gaining a true glimpse of the nature of dogs. I was teaching obedience classes, doing alternative therapy work and competing with my dogs in several different venues. The combination of the above has allowed me to gain a very unique perspective into the canine mind.

I am currently an alternative therapist, obedience and rally instructor, AKC judge and CGC evaluator and still living with and loving my Danes-who continue to teach me daily about life, living, loving and training.

Other Books By The Author

Rock Solid Stays

Wonderful Weaves

Couch To Competition

PAT Testing To Pick The Perfect Puppy

Puppy Kisses To Partnership-Starting Giant Puppies For Performance

Photo Credits

Cover Photo:

Pg 17. Sp-HIT, UAg2,UCD Liberty's Keeper Of My Heart VCD2,AXJ,RAE2,CGC,TT, photo by Serious Photo, Steve Bull.

Pg 31. Sp-HIT Liberty's Jahari Heart CD,RE,CGC,TDI with Kim Morisette, photos by Joyce Guthrie.

Pgs 33-34. Liberty's Silmarillion with Mary Foster, photos by Joyce Guthrie.

Pg 35. Liberty's The White Rider with Mary Foster, photo by Joyce Guthrie.

Pg 37. Liberty's Silmarillion with Mary Foster, photo by Joyce Guthrie.

Pgs 49-50. Liberty's Silmarillion with Mary Foster, photos by Joyce Guthrie.

Pgs 52-53. Liberty's The White Rider with Mary Foster, photos by Joyce Guthrie.

Pg 58. Liberty's Mystique Reflection with Mary Foster, photo by Joyce Guthrie.

Pg 62. IntCh,UACH,UCD Liberty's Magic Touch UD,OA,AXJ,OAP,OJP,RAE2,CGC,TDIA,TT,ASCA-HIT, Joyce Guthrie, UAg2,UCD Liberty's Road To Rivendell CD,RE,OA,OAJ,NAP,NJP,CGC,TDI,TT/SP-HIT,UAg2,UCD Liberty's Keeper Of My Heart VCD2(CDX,OA,OAJ,TD)AXJ,RAE2,CGC,TT/Liberty's The Lgnd Returns/UAg1 Liberty's Kindred Spirit CD,RA,NAP,NJP,CGC, photo by Mickey Rabeneck.

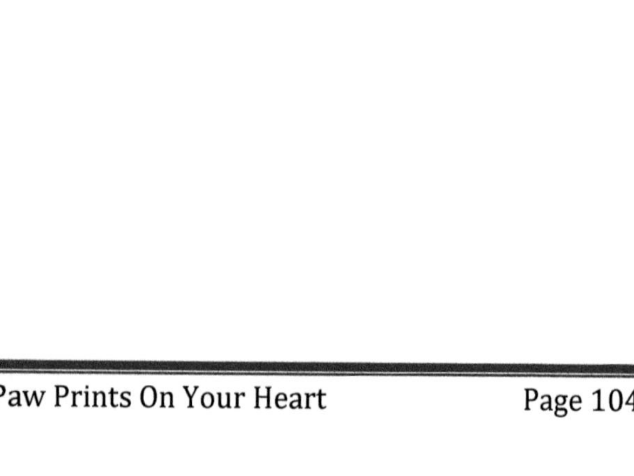

www.ingramcontent.com/pod-product-compliance
Ingram Content Group UK Ltd.
Pitfield, Milton Keynes, MK11 3LW, UK
UKHW020239250726
13967UKWH00001B/464